A map for the soul...
Compassionate journey...

Tjaatutjanun? Where are you from?

Mirek Woznica

WESTBOW
PRESS
A DIVISION OF THOMAS NELSON
& ZONDERVAN

WestBow Press books may be ordered through booksellers or by contacting:

WestBow Press
A Division of Thomas Nelson & Zondervan
1663 Liberty Drive
Bloomington, IN 47403
www.westbowpress.com
1 (866) 928-1240

ISBN: 978-1-4908-7384-8 (sc)
ISBN: 978-1-4908-7386-2 (hc)
ISBN: 978-1-4908-7385-5 (e)

Library of Congress Control Number: 2015904278

Print information available on the last page.

WestBow Press rev. date: 03/24/2015

Contents

To God, Who is the reason behind my life and this book.

To my inspiration and encouragement, my wife Regina, who once said: "You should write these things down", and was loving and patient with me as I did.

To so many, Angels in my life, who have crossed my path and touched my silly life.

To my dearest family and old time friends for their constant and unfailing love and support.

To You, who decided to read my story.

Praying with gratitude …

"May God grant me to speak as he would wish and conceive thoughts worthy of the gifts I have received, since he is both guide to Wisdom and director of sages; for we are in his hand, yes, ourselves and our sayings, and all intellectual and all practical knowledge".

(Wisdom 7:15-16)

ix

LUURNPA AND THE PROMISED LAND

The Luurnpa (kingfisher) made his home in the south. When he was tired of living and sleeping alone he decided to find somebody to sit down with him in his country and to sing songs with him and play corroboree.

One day he decided to get up and look around. He travelled north into the desert—northwards in search of his people. He kept on searching—and came back the same way, from the north, back southward, back to his home. He found no trace of any living being.

The next day he flew back northwards. He saw a little snake coming out of a hole no bigger than an ant-hole. The hole was so tiny that the Luurnpa could just fit his beak into it to make it wider. As he did this, he saw that there were people down that hole, but they were like stone. He knew that they had been there many years under the ground.

He breathed into the hole and they came to life. Then he sorted out which ones were strong ones who could follow him. The ones who were too weak he set aside to die. Then he said to the others: "Come with me. I need company. I am alone". And he took them to his own good country.

He led them from waterhole to waterhole, so they always had water to survive the long hot journey—water from the soaks and the rockholes. He looked after his people with water, kangaroo, goanna and lots of other bush tucker on their way.

While they were travelling, he looked back at his people and said to himself, "Oh, what a mob I've got! These people will be my people". Wirrimanu was the path the Luurnpa took, and he and his people settled down in Kukatja country, and the Luurnpa was happy.

Told by Marukurru Sunfly, the custodian of the story, through John Lee

Art Work by Matthew Gill, Balgo

Prologue

It has taken me many years to begin sharing on paper, namely writing about my experiences. My soul seems to take time digesting, analyzing and reconciling times and places, opportunities and encounters, relationships and circumstances. My reason tries to bring some balance into all of it, but does not always succeed. So after more than ten years I decided to share with you what God blessed and challenged me with in my life. This is just a humble first attempt.

Sometimes God sends us to places where He decides to meet us. If we choose to go where He wants us to be, there is a high possibility that we will meet Him somehow. One of the most amazing, and challenging, places where He led me was the Great Sandy Desert in the middle of Australia.

I was blessed to be there and completely honored to cross paths with the Aboriginal People and with the Aboriginal Dreaming, or Tjukurrpa. Some of the stories and encounters changed my life and some helped me to see and understand the meaning and purpose of my life. All of them have molded me into the person that I am today. I am sharing one of the many stories with you in this book and the lessons I have learned. I would like to invite you to join me on my mysterious journey sprinkled with some miracles.

My story begins at the very end of dry season, the time of expecting the rain to come. This time of the year, the desert is filled with anticipation. I would wake up every day and smell the air, look up in the sky and see if there is a sign of a cloud.

Do you know that you can smell the rain coming? You can feel it in your nostrils when the wind blows; the air filled with moisture. It is an amazing sensation. The community talked about inviting a rain maker to pray for rain, using his very old traditional dance to ask for the water. He dances for days to ask the heavens to send the water back to earth where it came from. And it always works. We long for rain as much as the dry and thirsty land. We need to be refreshed and for the land to be brought to life again. We are waiting for new life. There is the flirting between heaven and earth unfolding that brings fertile rain. There is the tension in the air mixed with hope and impatience. It is the time for miracles to happen.

Kutjungka, in Kukatja language, means coming together as one family. Kutjungka Region in the Great Sandy Desert is made of five Aboriginal Communities: Wirrimanu which is named by white people Balgo Hills, Malarn named Mulan, Kururrungku named Bililuna, Kundat Djaru named Ringers Soak, and the former community of Yagga Yagga, abandoned by its 47 community members at one time after a devastating young boy's suicide and a long sorry time. These communities also make up what is known as the Tjurabalan Communities. The main language groups are Walmatjarri, Kukatja and Jara. The families have relatives all over the desert, and they travel to visit with them. Their departures and arrivals in the community are most of the time "spur of the moment" decisions, which means whoever shows up in the community with a working vehicle becomes a potential "travel bus". Travelling on foot is rare these days, but it does happen. Time is a space filled with travels and meetings. Time is measured by the sunrises and sunsets in the desert therefore the destination could be enjoyed much longer. Sometime they stay for weeks and sometimes for months at a time. As their ancestors travelled all over the country following the patterns of the nature, finding food and shelter, so now do the people of the desert. There is a lot of travelling during the dry season because every place is accessible by road. During wet season, the travels are often compromised by the flooding of the roads and hard driving conditions. But this is another story for another share time.

The people of Kutjungka call the Creator and God "Mama Kankarra," which means Father up above, Father in heaven. I was their Mamangku, which means the representative of Mama Kankarra with them. I was their friend, confessor, driver, and companion. I was their priest. I travelled a lot to visit with the families because I was one with them and one of them—Kutjungka—coming together as one. I travelled between communities to provide spiritual guidance as well as to share God and my faith. I was the only priest at that time for the region, which meant a lot of driving and visiting. I am sharing with you just one special time when I decided to visit a remote community far away from where I was stationed.

Early on Sunday afternoon as I was coming back from Kururrungku on Tanami Road, two aboriginal women with a few children and one older man were sitting behind their vehicle. As I got closer I recognized their faces. They were from Balgo. It looked like they had been there for a while, hiding in the shade created by the car. The children were asleep and the adults kept watch, looking for a lift back home. After living for a while in the desert you learn quickly that sometimes it can be a matter of life and death when you see a scene like that. I stopped to ask what happened and if everything was good. They answered "Palya", which means good. Their car broke down and they needed a lift home. They all jumped in, and off we continued together towards

Wirrumanu. During the trip, we shared stories and listened to music. I learned from them that there were some people in one of the communities far south that would like to see me sometime; some of them were their relatives. I already planned to go shopping in Alice Springs that coming week, and I promised to try to visit them. I went shopping every two months because of the distance, 840 km, and the time it took. I did plan to go sometime during the week. As we turned from Tanami onto Balgo road, we noticed thick, dark clouds starting to come fast, blown by a strong wind. We felt the rain; we sensed the joy of the land.

Just as we arrived in Wirrumanu, the rained started to pour down. It was a warm and refreshing rain. I dropped them off at their place in the bottom camp and after saying a quick goodbye, I headed to my place. It was wonderful to get soaked with Mama Kankarra's blessing from above. I unpacked the car, brewed some coffee and sat down to watch and listen to the rain, while enjoying my coffee. All of a sudden, a restless feeling came upon me, and a voice in my soul, saying "You should depart now. Do not wait a few days. Get ready and travel". I tried to reason with the voice and debate with it about this surprise departure. It was getting dark. I was hungry and tired. This place was miles from away. But the more I tried to make some sense out of it, the louder the voice sounded in my soul.

Finally, I gave in. I was on my way. I had visited the community once before, so I said to myself, "No worries, mate. You can do it even though it is getting dark". I planned to use the GPS system when I came closer to the community.

After what felt like long hours of driving in the rain and dark, I tapped in the community name, which the system recognized. Things were going well and I was getting close, and the GPS system did indeed direct me off the so-called "main road" onto the back roads. It looked familiar—bear left, turn right, turn left, and so on, until after a while it said "After 400 meters you have reached your destination", followed by, "You have reached your destination". Only I hadn't.

It was pitch black, pouring with rain, and I appeared to be somewhere, but not where I wanted to be. I had to find a map in the car and work out where I needed to go. I found the map... then I was stuck. Maps are useful, but only if you know where you are—which I didn't. I knew where I had come from, and I knew where I was going. I had just got lost along the way.

The night was dark and the clouds slowly moved to the west. The rain and the wind stopped and the most amazing display of the stars and full moon appeared in the sky; It was the most amazing painting reflecting the beauty of the Creator. God blessed me with the perfect place to stop. It was time to set up a little camp and light a fire, it was time to rest, and, as I learned soon, it was time to communicate.

By Mirek 'Tjangala' Woznica

How We Relate ...

I got out of the car and immediately was reminded of some good advice from a friend of mine called George of the Desert. He told me "You should always carry a lot of water when you travel through the desert, even if it's raining. When it is hot in the desert, your life could end as quickly as five hours or you might survive a day or two. Rainy days are much more merciful. You might need the water or someone else might. Water equals life. You should also carry some other important things that might help you survive or be used to help others; tools to fix your tires, tools for digging and so on. You think about others when you set out for a journey because sooner or later you your path will cross others' paths."

On this very night the air was fresh and the temperature was just perfect to enjoy the unexpected camping. The desert at night is mysterious and unpredictable, it is beautiful and frightful. The sounds of moving creatures and sneaky wind that caresses the bushes and the soft sand in the darkness appear to arrive from different directions. The time before your senses adjust to the sounds and the darkness can be very tense. After gathering a few sticks and lighting a little fire, I sat down on the ground. I unwrapped a sandwich and poured some coffee that I had brought with me. Coffee smells so good in the desert.

And as I was ready to take the first sip, I heard a question "Would you mind if we join you?" I jumped up, completely puzzled, but the voice sounded very peaceful and I did not feel afraid.

I waited to see who was there, but the person stood at a distance waiting for my answer. Hesitantly, I said, "Yes, please". There appeared to be two people. They came over and sat down with hats on, and their faces covered with the darkness of the night, but I knew by the confidence with which they walked that they were the people of this land: an old man and a boy.

As I gathered some more food from my bags and filled the billycan with water, the man sent the boy to collect some more sticks for the fire. As I came closer, the man said, "Words do reveal the heart and mind, but even more do the words we call gestures, actions and doings. It is most helpful to remember that not all of our words and deeds are purely of God; we have much of self that is in process. We cannot mean, sometimes, the things we say and we have the vocal power to reverse the injury by other words which we do mean. It is more difficult not to mean the actions we perform.

"Deeds and actions flow easily from the goodness within. 'From the fullness of the heart, the mouth speaks.' We communicate who we are all the time. We never stop. When we stop speaking, our body talks and every part of our being continues speaking".

"You did not see us walking in the darkness so I had to use a good voice and soft words to communicate peace and love, because darkness could be unpredictable and scary. We saw you in the light of the fire and you seemed a good man, but with no peace in your heart. Now that you can see us up close in the light of this fire, and you are able to listen to my words and body, we can speak to one another".

"It is like the story in Luke's gospel, I guess" I mumbled, confused by the unexpected wisdom, "A good tree does not bear rotten fruit, nor does a rotten tree bear good fruit. For every tree is known by its own fruit. (Luke 6:43-44a). We learn about others by listening and watching them".

He said, "What God is asking of us is to begin watching how much of Him is in us and how our gestures reveal Him. We are "inside-out" people. You see, I ask my boy sometimes to watch his tongue because he enjoys too many movie pictures and does not understand what some words mean and how they can affect others. The person who speaks the word carries the meaning of the word. What if you do not understand the meaning and yet use the word? Would others learn the full and right meaning behind the word?"

He paused, and I was surprised by his flow of words.

"Did your parents ever tell you to 'watch your tongue' and you tried to do it?" he continued. "I mean, stick your tongue out and try to look at it. That is not so easy to do physically, and just as difficult to do verbally. It is even harder to watch our actions, our body language, but we ought to do it. We help, love, lift up, console and reconcile through communication and we also hurt, bring down, divide and kill. It is a gift from up above that we choose how to use".

The boy returned with some sticks to keep the fire going.

I decided to tell a story I had heard about a young lay missionary who was carefully picking her way through the killing fields of Rwanda.

"She met a boy whom she knew was in one of the missions. He had witnessed his parents, brothers, and sisters being hacked to death by rampaging terrorists. He told her he no longer believed Jesus was God. She asked why. He replied, 'If Jesus is God, He should be able to do the things that God does. God made the trees and the trees make other trees. God made elephants and the elephants make other elephants. Now, if Jesus is God, He should be able to make other Jesuses. Yet I have never seen another Jesus".

The old man said quietly, "It is a sad story and I feel compassion for that boy. I pray for his comfort and peace. Awful things do happen to many people and our world is not free from cruelty and evil. I have seen and witnessed a lot in my life and still believe that we live in a bright world, a world made holy beyond all imagination. We move in the company of a sacred people. There is goodness about us that should be recognized and celebrated. The more we celebrate goodness, the more love and peace it will bring for others. If by any chance that goodness is not yet complete, well, it will be. If there is still a lot of darkness and shadows, scary places in your soul you do not want to be; listen to the angels and find the light. Light has taken a human form. That Light is God's love. Not a soul who believes in this Light should ever visit dark places anymore. Not a person shall ever fear to move towards the Light and feel safe and loved. In a world where terrible things happen there is a great need for compassion and safe places to rest the distressed souls."

The boy added, "I do not know what I would say or do, if I witnessed the killing of my loved ones in a brutal way. I have been blessed in this sense for not witnessing horror like that. I have also learned how to, on my own personal scale, deal with scary and fearful things. I learned that "monsters and shadowy, scary creatures", darkness with its false power are the things from my trembling dreams, no more than that. I learned not to let darkness overpower my hopes and dreams. I learned to remember but forgive. I do not fear them. I learned to grab them and bring them to the Light. They will not survive there. Try it sometime".

It reminded me somehow of (Luke 2:15-17) "When the angels went away from them to heaven, the shepherds said to one another, 'Let us go, then, to Bethlehem to see this thing that has taken place, which the Lord has made known to us'. So they went in haste and found Mary and Joseph, and the infant lying in the manger. When they saw this, they made known the message that had been told them about this child".

"We thank you", the old man said, "for sharing your food with us. These are delicious sandwiches and your coffee tastes so good". He added, "Those who are wealthy must be generous with their wealth. Those who have no money at all, but have time, talent, strength, insight, virtue, wisdom, they must be generous with that. It is not the wealth that matters. It is the virtue with which it is used".

"I have been helped many times in my life", I responded, "so I try to share what I have. But not always. I feel like the rich man sometimes, being blessed in abundance and not sharing the blessings, being gifted and not sharing the gifts, having necessary resources and not sharing them with others".

The old man quoted (Luke 16:30-31): "He said, 'Oh no, father Abraham, but if someone from the dead goes to them, they will repent.' Then Abraham said, 'If they will not listen to Moses and the prophets, neither will they be persuaded if someone should rise from the dead.'". And he added, "We are the hands and feet and mouth and eyes of the Living God".

"It is true", I agreed. "A poor man attended parish gatherings for months. He was totally ignored. One day he deliberately left his hat on. An usher was sent to him by the pastor. The poor man said, 'I thought that would do it. You are the first person from this community to speak to me in six months.' I do fail to see with virtue; I see with rigid eyes", I finished.

"We are all Mama Kankarra's kids. We are all the same. We belong together", the old man shared. "Wealth can be very deceptive. It can give us a picture of ourselves and of one another that simply isn't true. Prosperity can build in us the illusion that we are self-sufficient, that we are independent, and that others should be so as well. Being able to fulfil and satisfy every need and almost every desire and wish can give us the foolishly false impression that it is only right that we should always be satisfied. The man stood up to stretch his old legs, and continued. "The truth is that Tjiitju (Jesus) doesn't care if a person is rich or not. This is not His concern but how those riches affect one's life is. The illusion of self-sufficiency, of independence, is a dangerous attitude and way of living. It may stop us from hearing and seeing the needs of others or the warnings of God in our day-to-day lives. It could blind us and prevent us from seeing and living the reality.

He paused and looked at me.

"None of us is independent in anything that matters. We are very much dependent on one another. We depend on your food and welcome, and you depend on our company to wait for the new day; and as we share our dependency we learn and grow. That is the way God made us, and it is the way He expects us to live. We are interdependent and intertwined; spiritually, emotionally and economically".

"Interdependent!?" I caught myself repeating. "I am an independent individual and I do not need anyone", I said loudly, to my complete surprise.

As I sipped my coffee, I grew amazed with the old man's words of wisdom. But it was more than just the words. There was something beyond his words entering my soul and reorganizing the inner me. I did not like it, even though I could not stop it at that time. I asked the man, "Have you learned these wise things from your old, strong culture?"

The man smiled and answered, "There are so many little things from my past that I remember; the smells of my grandmother's cooking, the tastes of a special event's meals, the traditions, the flavors of bush tucker, and so on. I remember the ceremonial dances and late night stories flavored with laughs or arguments, I remember the tastes of freshly cooked goanna (*Australian monitor lizard*) that someone shared with me. Each one of us cherishes these memories in our hearts. I think it is good for us to be reminded from time to time how powerfully influential family ties really are. We are all one family; you and I are family, all the people in the world are family. You and I come together in this region called Kutjungka as one.

"We learn many skills as we grow up. In my opinion, one of the most important skills that we learn is the ability to initiate and maintain human relationships, the skill of understanding and growing together, that skill that helps you to sit and enjoy each other's company even after a silly fight that just happened. I remember one time the government decided that we needed bicycles in our community to exercise and have fun, so they shipped about 20 kid's bicycles. It was hard to decide who gets one and who does not, so the community encouraged us kids to share. Well, at least the community *tried* to encourage us. There were about 60 or more kids at that time in the community and as you can imagine, about the same number of daily fights over the bicycles. We would fight during the day and sit to have a meal near the fire at night to share stories and company. Finally, some of the bicycles got broken and some ended up on roofs where adults decided to keep them for the sake of peace and quiet.

I bet we all could share stories like that. No matter where life takes us, those early lessons still color and influence our interactions with others, even how we view ourselves. And it means that family members must be very careful with one another. It tells me that I have to be gentle and nurturing. It is from and through our family relationships that we get the things we need the most in our lives, namely confidence, support, affection, discipline, encouragement and even conflict. Conflict teaches us how to dislike from time to time, without ceasing to communicate and love. Family is the first place where we learn how to argue, and to deal with differences effectively and creatively, in a healthy way. It is the time of molding who we are to become. But keep in mind that everybody is capable of growth and change, and with that our relationships should grow too".

While listening to the old man, my soul decided to wonder, "Don't we sometimes do things just because we have always done them? Do we keep repeating things, calling them traditions, without even thinking how they fit in today's world?"

The boy said, "Each year his parents went to Jerusalem for the feast of Passover, and when he was twelve years old, they went up according to festival custom." *(Luke 2:41-42)*. If He did not go and they did not follow their custom, His parents would not have learned about His wisdom as He shared in the temple. In Kutjungka, when a young boy comes to a time when he is ready to become a man, he follows the old tradition of this land and learns from the elders what it means to be a man. He learns about hunting, traditions, and many other things. We call it Law. He follows the old ritual in order to grow and learn. I do follow the tradition in order to learn and grow, not merely to fulfill the requirement of my age. I do what for many generations young men in this region had done. It is our tradition, it is our culture, it is our strength," finished the boy.

What We Create ...

I felt that it was good time to ask where they came from so I said, "The world may in terms of technology be the 'global village' described by Marshall McLuhan some 40 years ago, but it no longer is a 'global village', connected emotionally. I have a feeling sometimes that what Jesus was sent for does not happen anymore". And I quoted Luke 4:18, "'The Spirit of the Lord is upon me, because he has anointed me to bring glad tidings to the poor. He has sent me to proclaim liberty to captives and recovery of sight to the blind, to let the oppressed go free.' And if you look around it is so hard to see it".

Before I could ask the question about where they came from, the old man looked deeply in my eyes and whispered, "I heard your question before you even thought about asking me. This is a question that I would like for you to answer this very night. Tjaatutjanun? (Where are you from?) Do you still remember where you came from?"

I looked at him, surprised. I was speechless while he continued. "We live in a world of separated communities, clubs and organizations with a clear movement to smaller, more definable groupings of similar people. We divide ourselves in so many ways: sports teams, political parties, denominations, economic status, high school attended etc. Our immanent world has become too small to reach fulfilment, so we struggle in relationships that are not definable, not at all manageable, and those relationships demand a constant broadening of our personal horizons. Each of them demands emotional, spiritual horizons as broad as God's own.

"And do you know what the saddest part of it is?"

I was deep in thought, but I tried to listen intently.

"It is that when we choose a smaller world to live in, we think it will be more manageable, but instead it becomes our prison cell. A prison cell, after all, is small and manageable. And, for some people, after a while, this is familiar enough to be comfortable.

"Yes, Jesus promises to open the doors to our cells but He doesn't promise to drag us out of them. When you think about community, there are certain signs and qualities that come to mind. People join communities for various reasons and they leave them for different reasons as well".

"If I may add this", I interrupted again. And without waiting for his response, I said, "Applying this to our church community I believe we can say the same thing. People emphasize different qualities that constitute this or that particular church. Some focus on the social mission, some on sharing the Good News, some on helping the less fortunate, and so on".

As I was about to continue he gently said, "I do not like when you interrupt me. Please do not do that. No matter how important it is that you need to say, it can wait. Listening is a skill that shows respect toward others. Now, let me refer to your last statement.

"It is very tempting to judge or compare in order to understand any community, even church community. We have to resist the temptation to do such things because we may be stopping God's graces from working through and within communities of people. We might be pushing God away from this community and replacing Him with our ideas what a community of people of faith should work like, look like, or simply be like.

"Kurrunpa (Holy Spirit) works in mysterious ways. The work of God on earth and with us is not finished; let us keep that in mind. It is a process that includes a lot of changes in the meantime. God is not done yet!"

And while he was still speaking I heard the voice in my head, "Do not be afraid any longer, little flock, for your Father is pleased to give you the kingdom". (Luke 12:32)

When he paused, I added, "There are times when I ask questions about the end times. There are a lot of people that seem to be concerned about the details that proceed and how it will happen. They questioned Jesus about that too. Then they asked him, 'Teacher, when will this happen? And what sign will there be when all these things are about to happen?' (Luke21:7) "We worry and live in fear of something, but we are not sure why. Are there any answers? How to prepare ourselves? Are our communities helping us to be prepared?"

The boy said, looking at us, "Let me answer this. I have lived all my life in the community; I have learned to relate to others, by which I mean, have relationships with other people. I have my brothers and sisters, cousins and uncles and aunties and mums and dads, grandfathers and grandmothers; I have my future spouse choices and future family options. I have a complex kinship system where everyone is related to everyone else. I know my place and my relationships with others. I belong to family. The kinship system has been passed from generation to generation in order to help us understand where and how we belong. Every relationship enriches me and challenges me at the same time. Most often, getting through the day as virtuously as I can is a pretty spectacular and dramatic thing; a demanding thing, calling on the best skills and strengths I have to offer.

"Doing all of my daily chores and routines and doing so patiently, charitably, joyfully, is quite an accomplishment, as is trying to fit in with the community and become the best I can.

"That is a challenge so often. A time when I would like to go and play might be a time when I have to learn a valuable lesson from my community, or a skill from someone whose path I cross. I have to make a choice every time to be part of the community or to do what pleases me. I do choose to build relationships or I choose to fill my instant desires. I do not have to attend the sorry business because I am still a boy. There is a fun footy game going on right now between the communities. It is a great fun for kids. When my uncle asked me to go with him I said 'No' but after a day I reconsidered and I am on an interesting journey learning a lot of things. I am grateful I am here".

The old man took over from there. "You can understand yourself and grow as a person only by living with and relating to one another, by building and maintaining relationships with kindness, respect, sensitivity, compassion, by faithfully and trustingly living in the presence of God, and by living in the community. So let us act that way. I believe that we don't need to look for complicated, mysterious plans for the coming of the new things or to prepare for the end times. We do not have to live waiting for anything of that sort. If you spend your life living within the community God has given you, and you try to make a difference every day of your life, then you are on the right track. That is the good way; to focus on now, with the wisdom of the past and hope of the future".

"I think I understand it more now", I said. "The way is clear. The direction is simple". And I remembered some other words I read in the past by Pierre Teilhard de Chardin: "We must renew in ourselves the desire for the great coming, and live desire daily till it happens', and Vincent McCorry's words, 'What matters is not the timing but the fact.'

Growing In Wisdom ...

The fire kept us warm and comfortable, and with some food in my belly I felt relaxed and safe having company. I completely forgot about the fact that I was lost somewhere in the desert. I asked the old man why he asked me the question, "Where are you from?"

He sighed and answered, "In the Bible, the one who has faith is the one who is faithful, who keeps trying, and who never quits. And that makes a world of difference. A believer doesn't make blueprints. A believer doesn't presume to decide for God what should happen, when it should happen, and how it should feel.

"The call to faith is not a promise of a life made free of challenges, obstacles, and burdens by the power of God. It is not a promise of a life that always makes sense. It is not a promise that life is always marked by clear purpose and satisfaction. Rather, it is a call to "keep at it", even when there is mystery, even when life does not make sense. It is a promise that precisely in that perseverance is the power of God. The power of God doesn't always have to feel divine in order to be so. And when I saw you by the fire I felt you had lost your faith. You want to control and understand, you want to make no mistakes because you have no desire to learn from them. You thought that "you have reached your destination", but you are not where you are supposed to be. You put your faith in things, like that thing in your car that tells you how to get places, and you also put faith in your own powers".

I felt my eyes filling with tears and prayed with the Apostles. "Increase our faith!" (Luke 17:5), knowing how right the old man was.

The wise old man went on, "There are so many people with great potential to achieve a lot, but because they lack faith in more than themselves, the words 'he has a great potential' will remain words and never turn into a real greatness. The skills will remain talk all of their lives instead of daily living force".

While listening to his words, I caught myself thinking that Walt Disney was right when he advised someone to "Quit talking and begin doing".

The man must have heard my thoughts, because he said, "I agree with the Mickey Mouse man. You should quit talking and start doing. You carry way too much from the past that does not allow you to have faith in God. The past is holding your faith and growth back. Let Mama Kankarra take care of your past. Have faith in Him that He can do a good job. He knows you deep down and inside out. These are not my words, but I like them: "Justice consists in finding out a certain thing due to a certain man and giving it to him. Temperance consists in finding out the proper limit of a particular indulgence and adhering to that. But charity means pardoning what is unpardonable, or it is no virtue at all. Hope means hoping when things are hopeless, or it is no virtue at all. And faith means believing the incredible, or it is no virtue at all". (G. K. Chesterton)

"What is holding me back? What do I carry?" I asked.

"Jesus was once entering a village. Ten lepers met him at the gate and wanted to be healed. He granted their request and sent them to a priest. Only one of them realized what happened and came back to express gratitude. He understood! He came back to the source of healing. His body and soul were healed. 'Then he said to him, 'Stand up and go; your faith has saved you.' (Luke 17:19) So many times we pray for good health, healing, recovery and many other immediate gifts from God. People go to various places with the need and expectations to be healed. Sometimes they are healed and sometimes they are not, they think, because they imagined it would feel or look different. Sometimes the outside healing makes them change their lives and sometimes it does not make any difference, but just gives them the feeling of being healthy again.

"You must be willing to accept the fact that God's response to your prayer is the best possible response, even if it doesn't fit your plans. And that is probably the most difficult step in any person's spiritual growth. It is the point at which we are called to go beyond our known experience, whether that is good, bad, or anywhere in between, and rely on God. Not because of what He seems to do for us, but simply because He is God.

"You have taken over your life from God's hands and tried to manage it by yourself, allowing Him from time to time to do some repairs; but you need a major work done on your life.

"I could compare your life to a puzzle. You have had a wonderful frame as a gift from God. Once you had all the pieces of your life puzzle. But you have lost some and exchanged others for pieces that are not yours. You have dropped some under the table and you've already forgotten about them. You have given some away for pleasures and instant fulfilment of your desires. You do not even try to finish the puzzle because you have lost interest in putting it together. But deep down in your heart there is the cry for the wholeness and the passion for life; deep down inside of your soul, there is the need to see the whole picture, but you have closed the door to this part of yourself and you think that it will die quietly. It will never die! It will never be quiet! It will never let you sleep at night peacefully and let you forget about the beautiful life that you could have had".

"But I do pray and I work hard to share God's word", I said in my defence, "and I know that faith is not stagnant but flowing, not still but requires movement, needs to be on a constant pilgrimage of the heart. Looking straight at the old man's face I continued, "That is why I am here in the middle of nowhere. Because I am trying to do God's work. I *am* trying"! I shouted and got up.

An awkward silence followed.

The boy broke the silence and said, "I understand your anger. I think we can identify ourselves with Martha's plea. We feel victimized at times. We feel like nobody cares and we are left alone to do "things". We feel resentment towards others and, yes, anger. Martha must have been a person who took her responsibilities very seriously—a person who realized that there is in life a certain amount of work that we have to do, and sitting around talking is not going to get it done. So she walked up to Mary and Jesus and said 'Lord, do you not care that my sister has left me by myself to do the serving? Tell her to help me.' (Luke 10:40) At times we can build our resentment and even anger towards God".

The old man quietly added, "We can also identify with Mary who is more reflective. It means to be aware of reality, and to respond accordingly. Mary in the gospel was apparently more successful at that than was Martha".

I was getting less angry and decided to sit down again. I wanted to apologize but my stubbornness did not allow me to admit my fault. I sat down.

At this point the old man came with some more words.

"So in our busy, often hectic lifestyles we are invited, we are challenged, to integrate the Martha and the Mary in our lives: the active service of Martha that responds to the needs of others, and the contemplative being of Mary that gives God prime time".

"You have a lot of growing to do and reconciliation to attend to. You need your faith to be alive and to allow God to bring your peace and balance back. I think you can start with combining Martha and Mary together by learning what it means to Ora et Labora". (Latin 'Ora at Labora' means 'prayer and work', the ancient Rule of St. Benedict. Living a life of prayer and work is the basis of Benedictine life)

I sat there quietly, trying to remember the time when I lost my faith.

The silence was not awkward anymore but a necessary way to connect our hearts to the wisdom of the universe. We treated each other with love and respect and our words reflected that. We spoke to each other the truth with love and respect.

After taking a deep breath, I said, "He was praying in a certain place, and when he had finished, one of his disciples said to him, "Lord, teach us to pray just as John taught his disciples.' (Luke 11:1). Jesus did teach us how to pray, and we keep repeating the prayer, adding more words and creating more prayers. I have memorised a lot of them and I speak from my heart with God. But knowing how to pray and seeing the results of our prayers are two different things".

At this point I felt like talking to the universe within me, trying to understand the complexity of my life journey or find excuses for my past shortcuts. I did not know at that time:

"If God really does love me, why doesn't He answer my prayers?

"Why doesn't He take better care of His people?

"Why does He leave so many of them so hungry and so needy in every way; physically, emotionally and spiritually?

"I struggle to answer these questions and do not seem to find a way to improve my prayers without seeing the purpose of praying".

The boy, who was looking up at the beautiful starry sky, spoke to us.

"I believe we can find in our lives unanswered prayers for any of a million things. I have talked with Mama Kankarra about many things; I believe that is prayer. I just want God to know what is in my heart.

"When you talk to someone you trust and you know you are loved unconditionally, you do not expect the person to do things for you. You speak your heart out because you know that if there is anything he can do for you, he would do it without being asked. I pray to God as to a friend I trust, that He, out of love for me, would do anything possible. I cannot get mad at Him if He does not give me the impossible".

While I was listening, my soul started singing quietly the prayer that Jesus taught us:

> You are our Father, you live in heaven,
> We talk to you. Father you are good.
> You are our Father, you live in heaven,
> We talk to you. Father you are good.
>
> We believe your word, Father,
> We are your children, give us bread today.
> We believe your word, Father,
> We are your children, give us bread today.
>
> We have done wrong, we are sorry,
> Teach us, Father, all about your Word.
> We have done wrong, we are sorry,
> Teach us, Father, all about your Word.
>
> Others have done wrong to us,
> And we are sorry for them, Father, today.
> Others have done wrong to us,
> And we are sorry for them, Father, today.
>
> Stop us from doing wrong, Father,
> Save us all from the evil one.
> Stop us from doing wrong, Father,
> Save us all from the Evil One.

You are our Father, you live in heaven,
We talk to you, Father, you are good.
You are our Father, you live in heaven,
We talk to you, Father, you are good.

The old man chimed in. "I also believe for some of us these questions could be a stumbling block. If God doesn't answer prayers, if prayer makes no difference in one's life, then why pray? And when prayer ceases, then faith follows very shortly and hope dies.

In our day-to-day lives, we create and surround ourselves with things, feelings, emotions, stories, and people that we want. Therefore, we allow them to enter into our lives. There is a big difference between these and the things, feelings, emotions, stories and people that we *need*. I think that is the most important in understanding why we should pray with trust in God.

"Our Father knows what we need, and if we are only expressing what we want it is not necessarily the same thing. If we could only refocus our prayer, take away the focus from "me, us" and turn our attention to God, we might find the answers.

"When I focus on what is far away on the horizon, I always stumble upon sticks and rocks. If I watch my steps I can see ahead and at the same time avoid dangers and stumbling. It is now, not in the future, that you walk, so watch where you put your foot now. 'God is not someone who grants our wishes; He is someone who fulfils our hopes'". (Anthony Padovano).

The boy continued. "When I was younger, I had many toys. I would ask Tjiitju to give me the toys the other kids had, and in time the angels who heard me allowed that to happen. When I look back, I feel sorry for destroying and throwing away my toys after just one day of playing with them. I would ask for something else, play for a while and get another one. Kids are very spoiled in our communities for so many reasons. One day I went with my family to another community far away in the desert where my aunties live. They had big mob of kids there. They had no toys, and I learned to play with other kids and not toys. It is more fun and you get to know them. You cannot destroy or throw away a kid after you play with him or her. You learn how to get along, which is a useful gift".

"When we grow up", said the old man, "we remember those lessons. We remember that we are responsible for what we have been given: either toys or people. We are reminded of being part of one family under one Love.

"When I was little I would get in trouble many times. One time I stole a boomerang from an old man. I wanted to play with it. I did not know that the boomerang was for the ceremonies. The old man looked everywhere and asked everyone. I did not want to get in trouble so I said nothing. I hid it in a Rockhole. After a while, he said nothing, and I thought I had got away with it.

"A few months after that, when I was getting ready to become a man, I needed approval from an old men. So I talked to my grandfather and some old men. One was the man I had stolen the boomerang from. He told me he knew who stole his boomerang. I asked him, 'Who'? He said to me that he would tell me in a week's time. During that week, all boys who were coming of age went into the desert to learn about our way, to learn our culture and how to live it and respect it. What I learned during this week was to make good choices, because every choice has its consequence in the future.

"I did not become a man that year. I had to wait until the next year because I did not show that I was responsible as a person. At first I felt like a victim. I felt I did not deserve to wait another year. I was ready for it and I was angry about not being able to go ahead and join the men. It was only later that I accepted the consequences and took ownership of my weakness. First I told my grandfather about the boomerang and we met with the old man together while I confessed and told the truth. Now I was ready to become a man. I was given a gift of speech and I used it to deceive and lie instead of telling the truth. I also learned in my short life that when dealing with my failure or hardships, or simply hard times in life's circumstances, I must refuse to be victimized, refuse to be powerless, no matter what the circumstances. It means that I honestly look at my life, clarifying what matters and what does not, and then assuming control, assuming responsibility.

"I think there is an old word that sums it all up, and the word is stewardship. It means to make the best, the most successful, use of whatever we have been given. Successful use of our resources is measured by the goals we have set. If those goals are being realized, the concrete choices we make in day-to-day situations are well set. But if those goals are not being realized, if we are not moving any closer to what we hope to be, then it is a pretty safe bet that it is time to take a little closer look at what we do… day to day, moment to moment. It is time to assume responsibility and control".

"What you shared reminds me of two messages from the holy books", I responded. "'We are born with our hands clenched. We die with our hands open. Entering life, we desire to grasp everything. Leaving the world, all that we possess slips away,' says the Talmud". And, 'the person who is trustworthy in very small matters is also trustworthy in great ones; and the person who is dishonest in very small matters is also dishonest in great ones.'" (Luke 16:10)

The boy was still gazing up at the greatness of the sky. There are no city lights in the desert. The display of the majestic stars is stunning and the experience is unique. As he was looking up he asked, "Do you trust that all these amazing things are created out of love for us, and that all the promises will be fulfilled?"

"Blessed are you who believed that what was spoken to you by the Lord would be fulfilled". (Luke 1:45) I said, proud of myself to answer with certainty.

"I asked if you do, not what the book says", the boy responded sadly.

The old man stood up and said, "Hope is a virtue. In many places, many times it was hope that kept human spirit alive. Stories have been shared in all corners of the world about how hope in something or someone brought the expected outcome. People lived through to see the expected. But sometimes the expectations of what the hope should look like could take away the true fruit of the hope that comes as it pleases. 'When this person comes, or that event happens, then our lives will be changed; things will be better', we say to ourselves, and we wait and wait until it happens our way.

"When you saw clouds coming a few days ago you expected rain. Not because you had hope, but because you have learned that if there are clouds there must be coming rain. I am not talking about that kind of trust in what we know and understand. I would like to talk about the trust that is hard to understand, and to know when the unexpected is coming.

"You mentioned Mary, Jesus' mum. Mary was great hope dressed in a body. She did not 'hope for', but she 'had hope'. She trusted God. Is it possible that this great hope for Messiah could look like a very young, very poor, very confused unwed mother? Is it possible that this ordinary girl could bring into this world this extraordinary gift? Her whole life was made up of entirely commonplace, everyday events. And that is a powerful revelation. No one's life is ever made important or valuable by the things that they accomplish, or by the things that happen to them. Hope in things to happen and people to arrive does not fix our lives. Hope with conditions cannot enter our lives because we have said to it, "Wait, I know what you should look like and this is not it". True hope is not attached to any conditions, and only when it is not can it change the ordinary into the extraordinary in our lives. Can you accept a hope that can change ordinary circumstances of your life into anything but extraordinary?"

"How do I do that?" I inquired.

"By exercising that hope", the boy uttered.

"You seem to understand the mysteries of the world and speak with the wisdom of the universe. Where did you learn these things?" I asked the old man.

"It is not my wisdom", the old man replied, "but your soul is ready to listen. Many people look for some extraordinary words and complicated sentences or advice. Life requires simplicity".

"I think", I said, "that in Jesus' time people expected from Him exactly what you said and missed the chance to join his ways. They expressed their expectations by asking John the Baptist questions before they met with Jesus. 'And the crowds asked him, 'What then should we do?' He said to them in reply, 'Whoever has two tunics should share with the person who has none. And whoever has food should do likewise.' Even tax collectors came to be baptized and they said to him, 'Teacher, what should we do?' He answered them, 'Stop collecting more than what is prescribed.' Soldiers also asked him, 'And what is it that we should do?' He told them, 'Do not practice extortion, do not falsely accuse anyone, and be satisfied with your wages.' (Luke 3:10-14) After hearing from John the Baptist who announced His arrival, they left disappointed. Their expectations were not met".

"His answers sound so ordinary and obvious. It does not sound attractive or adventurous at all", the old man replied.

I decided to share more, so I continued. "There was a time in my life when I only expected to do great things. I felt like doing the ordinary things was a waste of my time. I defined things as ordinary by my own standards. I missed a lot of opportunities and blessings. I had a false image of God and of my role in His plan".

The boy, who was listening intently because the truth was spoken, said, "The practical steps that we take, the day by day living are very often not the sort of things that catch our attention or stir up our sense of adventure. Not a very exciting plan, we think to ourselves. I can almost imagine me saying to John the Baptist, 'Hey John, it is all fine common sense advice, but when do I get to do those great things that change the world?' And I can hear him say to us 'Whatever it may be that makes up your lives, in all of it, there is greatness and blessing for you, if you live it *gracefully.*' I have a lot of ordinary things to do in my life as a young boy and I ask the heavens to help me do them gracefully", he bowed his head in prayer, allowing the heavens to bless him.

"You asked me", I said, "Where I come from. I come from a far far away land, a land that has four seasons. I travelled here by plane and drove down to the desert in this vehicle. I came here from a different culture and language. I followed the path of a gardia people (white people). When I came here I crossed my path with your mob, your people. I was given a skin name, Tjangala, and became part of the larger family. I do appreciate it and I do struggle with it. I struggle with being in between two ways of life. I need to understand which way is better for me".

The old man said, "He replied to him, 'Friend, who appointed me as your judge and arbitrator?' (Luke 12:14). And who appointed me as a judge between different ways of life? Life is often described as a journey. We do travel! We take things to help us on our journey, but we ought to remember not to take too much. Take only what is necessary because the journey is long and we need the energy".

"What do I take for the journey? What do I pack and carry with me?" I asked with frustration because it all sounded so easy and I knew it was not. "When we plan a trip we prepare things that we believe we might need during our trip and at the destination. We also take into consideration how we will travel and all the limitations that come with it.

"I remember the time when I was packing my suitcases before leaving my home for the first time and flying to Australia. I was going to be here for five years. 'How do you pack your bags for five years?' I kept asking myself!

"I had to fit my "life" into two suitcases. It was tough to decide what I needed and what I wanted; what to take and what to leave behind. There were clothes that I liked, things that I was more attached to than others, memorabilia that reminded me of loved ones or held wonderful memories. I had to decide what to take but I could not take everything. How does one decide?"

"First you wanted me to be the judge between two different and equally important paths", said the old man. "Now you are sharing with me the luggage that you brought from your wonderful country. That is good. But it seems to me the things you pack and take with you are more important to you than who you are and what you take for the journey deep inside of you. Your heart is capable of carrying a lot of relationships with all feelings attached to them. Your mind is filled with knowledge, memories and words to cheer you up when you are lonely and rejected. You carry strengths and weaknesses. You move with burdens and luggage that is part of who you are.

"Some of those burdens and luggage belong to the past, but you have never dealt with them. You carry hurt and pain as well as joy and happiness. You are proud of the stories that make up your life. Stories of who you are, shared with others, as well as those stories that nobody has yet heard. All of them are part of who you are. Only when you realize that it could be too much to carry, you ask God to help you deal with what has been your responsibility. God does not take responsibility for your relationships. They are yours to take care of. God gives you the strength and courage to sort out your "spiritual luggage". Whatever path you take or cross in your life, it is yours to own. Whatever "luggage" is accumulated during your path, it is yours to deal with. Do not carry unnecessary burdens and pains. Travel light! Choose the things you carry in your heart wisely to finish the journey. Carry things that make you and others happy on the way where you are heading. Travel united with the heavens and let the angels help you travel".

"A wise man once said", added the boy, "If you want others to be happy, practice compassion. If you want to be happy, practice compassion". Dalai Lama XIV

"Why do you say I do not travel light? What are the signs by which you judge this?" I insisted.

"I look up to the heavens and ask for love to be shared", replied the old man. "I look down on earth and seek the wisdom of the people who walked here before me. I look at people and try to see the love they carry and the wisdom they learn. Sometimes the answers are not clear but the way to get them is. And other times there are just statements and observations but no answers".

"I am a selfish old man who wants to learn from everything. I did not tell you these things because I judge you, but because I would love for you to know it, so the mistakes of the people are not repeated and the heavens and the earth could be united again. I share with you what is in my heart so that you and I grow closer, making Mama Kankarra smile down on us because He wants people to be happy and love each other. He rejoices in goodness and love". The old man looked at me with his brown eyes and continued. "I heard about a wise man who wrote: 'Cana, the first miracle, the compassionate one when Jesus joined not in human sorrow but in human happiness.' The Brothers Karamazov, Fyodor Mikhailovich Dostoevsky. And I liked it!

"Love deepens relationships and grows in true depth between people. Where true love exists, assumptions turn into understanding and trust and expectations are replaced by readiness to serve with love. Can you tell me what the significance of Cana is?

"It is a town in Jesus country". I answered. "Jesus was invited there with his mum and some apostles for a wedding, and 'when the wine ran short, the mother of Jesus said to him, 'They have no wine.' (John 2:3). Eventually Jesus turned water into wine. It is called the first miracle".

"I like that miracle a lot", said the old man. "But more than the miracle I like the way Jesus showed compassion to people with an ordinary need. It helps me love and trust Him even more".

I said: "Jesus at first turned down, or seemed to turn down her request. Mary was not upset or concerned. Quite the contrary! She turned to other people and instructed them to stand ready".

The old man, with a grin on his face, said, "Her faith and trust in the Christ remained firm and solid. Her relationship with her Son was based on God's art of love. She knew in her heart that He would not let the bride and groom be humiliated by the circumstances. Things happen in our lives, and I always remember that for God nothing is impossible".

At that time, my soul was filled with questions that I have never asked myself before: "Could it be that I take 'no' for an answer too often and too soon? Could it be that I have more faith and trust in my own self than in God? Could it be that I am afraid to gladly depend on others?"

The boy, who was sitting down, remarked, "I know my mum loves me very much. Whenever I disobey her I know she looks at me with love and that makes me change next time because I love her too. I know deep down in my heart that Jesus loves me too, and His changing, renewing power can fill the gaps and needs in my life. It can give to my life richness, a value I may never have thought possible. All I need to do is bring my problems to him with trust".

"How do you bring your problems to him?" I inquired.

"I believe God lives in every person. If I bring to you my worries and problems, would you send me to God? If I need your time and love, would you send me away saying that you are busy, and that you will say a prayer for me? I talk to God; I share with

Him my problems and worries. I pray, surrender my needs to Him with trust. This is how I bring my problems to God".

I remembered something similar from the Bible: "As the day was drawing to a close, the Twelve approached him and said, 'Dismiss the crowd so that they can go to the surrounding villages and farms and find lodging and provisions; for we are in a deserted place here.' He said to them, 'Give them some food yourselves," (Luke 9:12-13) and I decided to speak. "When I worked as a chaplain at Joondalup Hospital in Perth I met an older woman. She was bitter and angry, and at first she said things to me which were not very kind.

"One of the things that I did at the hospital was morning visits with people. One morning, after I had visited patients, talked with them, prayed and spent some time with them and their families, I entered a dark room. As I asked "How are you? Can we pray?" and introduced myself, I heard a voice coming from the darkness of the room sending me right to hell. The voice sounded tired and firm at the same time. Well, I had no intention to visit such a place, and I said so. I decided to stay and talk a bit. I asked few questions and after a few exchanged sentences, this is what I heard: 'I am dying. I have to stay here because I have no one to look after me at home. I have two sisters and a brother living close by. My brother lives about an hour from here with his family. He is very involved with his church and does a lot for the community. He is a lovely man. My younger sister lives about two hours from here. Very devout person and is also very involved with her church. She is one of the church leaders there. She is a loving and caring person. Both of them called me few times and offered their prayers, but because they are so busy they cannot visit me or care for me at their homes. My older sister lives about a six hour drive from here and is coming tomorrow to be with me as long as it takes. But she is not a great believer and I am not sure if she is a churchgoer anymore. She is taking some time off work to be with me. I am bitter and angry because I feel like I am competing with God. I feel angry with God because He is taking my brother and sister away from me when I need them the most.

'I await my death, questioning if I am too selfish or my loved ones are too caught up with religion.

'When you mentioned prayer, I sent you to hell because I need real people to talk to and listen to me. I need God here and now in flesh. I need His presence visible and touchable. I hope God will forgive me for all of this!'

"She died about three weeks later. Her surprised brother and sister arrived with their families to attend the funeral. I just understood the lesson now. I understood how easily we can use God as an excuse to not to be with people".

"I am very glad you decided to stay and talk to the woman. She needed to get it off of her chest and be free of that bitterness", the old man said. "You showed her love and kindness, and God was present through that process.

"There are two kinds of people: Those who always insist upon their privileges and those who always remember their responsibilities. Those who are always mindful of what other people owe them and those who never forget what they owe others. Your moral and spiritual growth can be measured by how much love you have for God and how you show it. How much love you have for other people and how you show it. When all things in which you take pride have passed away: love, and those you have shown love, will be all you will have left with you on earth and up in heaven".

. I said, "It's rather embarrassing to have spent one's entire lifetime pondering the human condition and to come toward its close and find that I really don't have anything more profound to pass on by way of advice than, 'Try to be a little kinder'". (Aldous Huxley) And I added "I know that Love never fails. (1 Corinthians 13:8) But knowing does not mean understanding and doing. Sometimes the journey between my brain and my heart is a long journey and takes too much time".

I got up and walked to the car to get the holy book, the Bible. When I came back I asked the man and the boy to pray with me. I said, "Could we read 1 Corinthians 13:1-13, replacing the word love with Tjiitju or Mama Kankarra, please. I need to pray with someone".

And as we read together the heavens rejoiced and the angels came down to listen, because we spoke the language of the angels at that very moment.

If I speak in human and angelic tongues but do not have Tjiitju, *I am a resounding gong or a clashing cymbal.*

And if I have the gift of prophecy and comprehend all mysteries and all knowledge; if I have all faith so as to move mountains but do not have Tjiitju, *I am nothing.*

If I give away everything I own, and if I hand my body over so that I may boast but do not have Tjiitju, *I gain nothing.*

Tjiitju *is patient,* Tjiitju *is kind.* Tjiitju *is not jealous,* Tjiitju *is not pompous, it is not inflated,*

Tjiitju *is not rude,* Tjiitju *does not seek His own interests,* Tjiitju *is not quick-tempered,* Tjiitju *does not brood over injury,* Tjiitju *does not rejoice over wrongdoing but rejoices with the truth.*

Tjiitju *bears all things, believes all things, hopes all things, endures all things.*

Tjiitju *never fails. If there are prophecies, they will be brought to nothing; if tongues, they will cease; if knowledge, it will be brought to nothing.*

For we know partially and we prophesy partially, but when the perfect comes, the partial will pass away.

When I was a child, I used to talk as a child, think as a child, reason as a child; when I became a man, I put aside childish things.

At present we see indistinctly, as in a mirror, but then face to face. At present I know partially; then I shall know fully, as I am fully known.

So faith, hope, love remain, these three; but the greatest of these is Tjiitju.

I noticed tears coming down the old man's face and my soul was in tears as well, so we parted. He walked with his head down, slowly disappearing into the darkness. I heard him singing. The boy was sitting down with his eyes fixed on the fire. I looked up to the stars and remembered, "You shall love the Lord, your God, with all your heart, with all your being, with all your strength, and with all your mind, and your neighbor as yourself". (Luke 10:27). Slowly getting up, I touched the boy's shoulder and walked away. With each step the meaning of the words started to touch my heart. Suddenly my soul was flooded with questions.

"Where do I come from and where am I going?"

"What kind of life works?"

"Who is my neighbor?"

"For whom will I be held responsible in the eyes of God?"

Those are just a few questions that I asked myself that bright, starry night, but do we not all ask them ourselves frequently?

In many places in the Bible there are questions with clear answers. Jesus very plainly answers them. There are no secrets, hidden clues, deep mysteries. All is clear. Happiness does not depend on some secrets. Jesus' message is simple, but what it implies can be difficult to act upon and complicated.

And that night I needed to wrestle with the message. I walked up to it and grabbed the first thought that came to my mind. If I start to ponder on my religious nature, I thought, I might be able to gain some understanding. It is very tempting and easy to build an image of ourselves as Christians who follow rules and regulations, who "enjoy the comfort" of rituals and complicated laws that take away our responsibility for free decisions and consequently for being responsible for God in our lives and the lives of others. Rituals, rules and regulations or even theological knowledge have no saving value.

I was getting more and more frightened of the words coming and the truth slowly revealing itself as more thoughts rolled into my soul and mind. I could continue to keep asking questions, but I was not ready for the answers. I wanted to understand more before facing the challenge of changes in my life that needed to happen. I needed the wisdom of the old man and the humble advice of the boy. I needed time to talk more, to ask questions and to hear the Word, and I hoped to see my visitors near the campfire upon coming back. That was the time when I started coming back to Light. It was the time of returning.

Humility ... Readiness To Learn

As I was walking back to the fire, I collected some sticks. We had time until sunrise to talk more. Travelling at night is very tiring and dangerous. The corrugated road is unforgiving in the darkness. Upon my arrival I noticed the old man and the boy sitting down and enjoying the warmth of the fire. I added some sticks to the fire and sat down.

Then I said, "Two people went up to the temple area to pray; one was a Pharisee and the other was a tax collector. The Pharisee took up his position and spoke this prayer to himself, 'O God, I thank you that I am not like the rest of humanity— greedy, dishonest, adulterous—or even like this tax collector. I fast twice a week, and I pay tithes on my whole income.' But the tax collector stood off at a distance and would not even raise his eyes to heaven but beat his breast and prayed, 'O God, be merciful to me a sinner'"(Luke 18:10-13).

I heard a strong voice deep down tell me to share more of my story. I continued. "When we put structure, rules and regulations above the spirit and the truth, we lose sight of God and who we truly are. We obstruct our view of others by the limitations of the structure. It could be religion, language, culture, a habit, a club or community, and it is associated with words like 'we have always done it this way', 'everybody knows how to do it', 'come and learn how it works', 'the church teaches so', 'the old people say so', 'you follow just because', and so on. I have done it so many times in my life. I have done it to myself as well as to others. I have tried to stop people from growing spiritually. I have frustrated their growth because they did not fit the frame of rules or they violated the regulations in my narrow understanding of them. I have attempted to cut them off from God because the frame was too tight for them, and in my opinion it would not look good on them, and for some reason I felt it would take some power off me. I have attempted to hurt people by imposing on them the rules and regulations which I did not always follow or understand".

My soul was getting heavy and my voice weakened. I fell silent. I knew my wrong from the past, and I started to feel the weight on my conscience. In this silence I heard angels coming down and holding me tight and felt the old man's hand on my shoulder. I heard the boy's sigh.

The old man spoke. "One has no respect for himself or others if he does not live with humility. Judging others by some external, unified rules does not show respect for others at all. Every person is unique and different and deserves respect for who he or she is. If you try to fit different people into one frame you show no respect. You need to have a modest view of yourself first in order to be able to help others. You do not help by judging them or by comparing yourself to them, but by showing them love and understanding. If you are meek and humble of heart you are ready to love. But humility is not a feeling. Humility is not an instant movement of one's heart. Humility is a virtue, and it is needed in our lives in order to step aside and see ourselves through God's eyes of love.

"Whenever we look at others and compare, judge, use as an example to feel better or simply look down on, we deprive ourselves of the truth that could set us free and the growth that is our path. 'A great many people think they are thinking when they are really rearranging their prejudices' (William James), and that does not take them far from their selfish ways.

"I recall one time when I was getting ready for the Law time, I was teaching young boys about humility. One of them came to me after I talked to them and said, 'I sure hope they get your point.'

"I have doubts if he understood the meaning of humility.

"We live in a world of comparisons. For some to feel important, they need to find those who are less important. For the good looking and handsome there are the unattractive ones to make them look even better, for smart there are stupid, for rich there are poor, for good there are bad, for black there are white, for Christians there are Hindu, for old there are young. Humility requires us to acknowledge who we truly are: God's children, with great qualities as well as limitations. We depend and rely on God's judgment and guidance rather than our own. We put God first in our lives. It is the meaning of humility and the only way to become who we can possibly be.

"Meekness of heart helps me to have meaningful relationships with others and not a daily competition about who is better, stronger, wiser, and so on. Mama Kankarra loves each one of us the same and promises to give us the same place to live forever".

The old man closed his eyes and continued what sounded like a prayer:

"How does it feel to know that in heaven we will be the same?

"How does it feel to know that it does not matter how strong or powerful or rich or beautiful you are right now, this is not what you will take to heaven?

"What does it take to realize that we are one, equal but uniquely beautiful in the same time?"

"Humility is not a popular word these days, is it?" he asked opening his eyes.

"Christ offers humility", I responded, "but I struggle to believe that it works in today's world of everything instant, in a world of getting stronger, becoming richer, getting ahead of others at school and at work. I struggle to believe it works even though I studied His words, 'Blessed is the one who will dine in the kingdom of God.' (Luke 14:15) and heard a wise man say 'True humility is not thinking less of yourself; it is thinking of yourself less.' (C.S. Lewis).

"I keep comparing, judging, and using others as examples to feel better about myself, to belong and to move up the society ladder. It does not change me inside but makes me forget for a while that I need to work on, namely becoming meek and humble of heart. I want to enjoy eternity with others and celebrate our differences, because differences are beautiful".

"We have in our community lots of kids who are losing their culture and sense of belonging", the old man started saying. "I worry for them. They roam at night, in the community, with their noses attached to plastic bottles filled with petrol. They walk around and sniff petrol. After a while their hearts close and their brains disconnect. They withdraw from families and community. Petrol sniffers grow into a very disturbed and broken image of who they are. They stay up all night and sleep during the day. They live upside-down lives. By destroying themselves they bring sadness and worry to their families and community. They are dying spiritually and socially. Their self-esteem reaches bottom and nothing can change that. What can one do to help or stop them?"

He paused and looked at the young boy.

Compelled to answer, the boy said: "There are glaring hard lights and glowing soft lights. The stars above are an amazing display of the greatness and wonder of creation. The fire in front of us gives such a soft, pleasant display. It keeps us warm and in its light we can see each other's faces as we talk. If I move closer to the fire you can see my facial expressions much better and our communication may have a better flow because seeing helps when you talk. If I lift my face up and look at the stars, the stars will reflect the light to show my face. Light helps us to see well. As much as it helps to see others it also helps to see one's own self.

"I sniffed petrol and walked in the darkness because I was ashamed and did not want people to see my face. I was one of them, I was a petrol sniffer. I did not want to be recognized so I hid in the darkness. I walked at night because no one took the time to bring the light closer to me when I could not do it by myself.

"The closer one gets to the light, the more things will be revealed. The old man brought the light of his patience and love and I started to see. The closeness is not something that happens. The closeness was my choice. I chose to get closer to the light, but I needed someone to show me the light with love and patience".

The boy continued. "There are many walking in the darkness because they have not chosen to get closer to the light. I am not afraid of darkness anymore because I know that there is a light".

"Is it the same as what Jesus told Simon?" I inquired. 'Put out into deep water and lower your nets for a catch' (Luke 5:4), but when you see what happens in the light, your shame and low self-esteem make you repeat after Simon, 'Depart from me, Lord, for I am a sinful man' (Luke 5:8) and you choose to go back to walk in the darkness?"

"It is how much you are open to the possibility of true and unconditional love", the old man said. "It is how open you are to change. It is how open you can be to Mama Kankarra and the light of truth and life. It is how in tune you are with your soul and mind, and how connected you are to the heavens and to the earth. It happens when you live with Kurrunpa, the Spirit, inside of you.

"I see it sometimes this way: When I drive a car, I listen to the radio. When I turn the radio off it becomes quiet. The radio is not electrically active. I assume that the radio waves are continuing and perhaps passing right through me, but I am not receiving them. The radio is off. You can change and learn if you decide to open up, and you may ask these questions:

"Is my soul in on or off mode?

"How can I receive His waves of grace and blessings?

"Am I prepared to see the details of my life and God's wonderful power and beauty?

"Am I ready to face the truth?

"Am I prepared to face the truth and change my old ways?"

I did not try to answer the questions right then, but I heard Augustine of Hippo's voice in my soul: "Christ says, 'Give me this fisherman, this man without education or experience ... it will be obvious that it is I who am at work in him.'" And I prayed quietly: "I am a weak man. Can I humbly submit my life to the Light and trust love again? Kurrunpa Palya, enter my soul and help me to be open and willing to learn".

The Darkness ...

I looked up and in the glow of the moonlight I saw dark and thick
clouds coming. The wind smacked the flame and caressed our
faces. It was a chill wind. Pieces of spinifex grass blew by. I decided
to get blankets from the car. When I came back the boy asked,
"Are you afraid of the desert? Many gardia are afraid. Are you?"

"I am not", I started. "I used to be, but I have learned from
your mob to respect it. I have camped and hunted, I have put mud
on myself to respect the water before going into the lake so the
water is kind and I will not be harmed. I respect the snakes and
other animals and the people who walked the desert for thousands
of years, so I am not afraid because I show my respect and the land
will respect me in return".

I wanted to continue, but all of a sudden the wind stopped.
In that short silence I heard something that is unexpected at
night. I heard a willy-willy coming. Usually a willy-willy is
created during a hot sunny day. A willy-willy is, in Australian
slang, the name for a dust devil, a whirlwind that picks up and
carries dust. They are usually harmless, but occasionally are big
enough to pose a threat to people or buildings. They always
leave everything full of dust after they are gone. I felt some sand
between my teeth; we looked at each other and, seeing the dust
devil coming fast, decided to just cover ourselves with blankets.
This one was moving fast and strong. I had to hold on to my

blanket; otherwise the willy-willy might snatch it up. It lasted for only a few minutes but it sure felt much longer. I peeked from under the blanket. Everything was dark and quiet. I decided to get up and so did the man and the boy. We were all covered with thick red desert dust. It was everywhere; in my mouth, my eyes, under my clothes; I itched. And there was no sign of our fire. It was gone. The sky was completely black and once again covered with clouds.

What a sudden change, I thought. I cleared myself of the dust, at least what I could, and heard the man and the boy dusting themselves off. I heard the man asking me, "Nyuntun palya? (Are you Okay?)" I answered: "Yuwayi, ngayurna palya". (Yes, I am good). The boy coughed and spit on the ground. I washed my mouth with some water I found in the darkness and passed the water to the man. I heard him gurgle and spit the water.

"We need to find some sticks and start another fire", the boy suggested. The old man, to my surprise, declined, saying "No, let us sit down and stay in the darkness for a while".

We all sat down. The old man said, "I would like to teach you something about the darkness and talk about its prince".

"Who is the prince?" the boy whispered.

"It is the prince of darkness, the master of destruction and deceit and the great liar", the old man answered and continued:

"How do you feel sitting here in the darkness?

"What is the purpose of darkness?"

The boy was quiet. I opened my mouth to answer, but the old man was not done yet.

"There are few different qualities and kinds of darkness," he said.

"There is a darkness that I control. I can close my eyes and create darkness. When I open my eyes, the darkness is gone and the light is welcome. There is no fear or anxiety attached to that darkness because I can control it.

"There is a different darkness caused by others. When someone puts hands on my eyes from behind and asks 'guess who?' or when someone blindfolds me for some other reason. The first scares some people even though it is friendly darkness—it can be fun. This kind of darkness takes the notion of fear that is not caused by the person; it depends on what relationship I am in with the person. If I trust the person, I am not afraid. If I do not trust, I suffer in the darkness and grow in fear. I do not control this darkness.

"There is another darkness that is caused by something unknown to me. This darkness brings fear because I do not know or understand the reason behind it. If I did not know that it was willy-willy coming I would have been very scared, but I knew it would not harm me. With darkness caused by unknown comes a question: Why?

"It grows enormously into a gigantic fear in my soul and mind. I worry because of the force behind it. I cannot control the darkness that is coming and going, and this brings fear.

"There is also a darkness caused by me, which I have little power over. I caused the darkness but cannot bring the light back. When I destroy the source of light I create darkness. I can smash some lights in the house or on the street or I can destroy the source of light in my soul. I am capable of smashing all the lights in my soul and living in the darkness, because after a while I cannot find and remember the light that was in my soul. It is the worst kind of darkness if I choose to live in it. I can choose to end it but I need to fight the prince of the darkness to win. This darkness is hard to control, but it is not impossible.

"The evil one is very smart and very real. The prince of darkness will lie to keep me in the darkness. He will lead me to believe that everything can be achieved in an instant and tell me that it could be mine, but will never tell me that I am in the darkness. Instead, he will make me feel good instantly and by lying and twisting the truth he will show me things as they are not. At that moment of temptation the only choice I have is to say no to the prince of darkness. Otherwise I lose every time I enter into his game. I must know that he is much more powerful and more intelligent that I am, and he is wittier and quicker than I, and I have to remember it".

"How about Jesus?" The boy's voice sounded from the darkness, "He met the prince of darkness and showed us how to handle the evil one".

"What story are you talking about?" the man asked, surprised.

"Mamangku, you tell us the story", said the boy.

"It was the time", I began, "when 'Filled with the holy Spirit, Jesus returned from the Jordan and was led by the Spirit into the desert for forty days, to be tempted by the devil.'" (Luke 4:1-2). There, in the desert, the evil one tempted Jesus. He applied his temptation to desires, fears, and opinions.

"The first temptation shows me how not to fall into the trap of bodily desires. If I want to grow spiritually I must master my body's desires first. It could be a lifetime task.

"The second temptation shows me how to live with no fear in order to respect others and know the truth. If I want to grow, I need to have a real image of myself and not to fear things that I do not know, or understand. Jesus knew who he was; therefore, he did not need to prove anything to the prince of darkness. Fearless life is a life of inner peace. I can overcome fear by knowing the truth.

"The third temptation shows me how to respond to duty and obligations and to the desire to make the world conform to my philosophy, religion, opinions, and ideas of how it should be. This is the greatest battle that occurs inside of me between my conscience, mind and body. The prince of darkness is trying to tell me that if I choose to live in darkness I will change the world or the world will change for me. It is my ego that believes it to be true, but my soul, which is much more than my ego, knows that it is a lie. Again, Jesus shows me how to reject this temptation and follow the Truth".

"This is one of the few places in the New Testament in which the devil is mentioned as an individual", said the old man. "It was not the image of the devil known in Jesus' time, yet the image of the devil was so very appealing and real".

"You are so right", I said. "It is the image of self-destruction at work, because this is what the devil is and what he brings into a person's life. He uses the only tool he has, and that is lies. We call the lies "temptations". We are tempted, as Jesus was. This is the devil's job description: to tempt. We have the ability to respond to this temptation. The more we practice saying 'no', the easier it is to resist temptation and the stronger we grow against the evil".

The boy asked, "What can we learn from Tjiitju? Can we win against the prince of darkness?"

"It is a powerful story", said the man. "I think that if at any moment Tjiitju had given in to temptation, all His work and His mission would have been jeopardized, and even finished before it began. If Tjiitju chose to go along with the devil's temptations, he would have been accepted instantly and used his powers in the worst way. He would have brought to people food and shelter and instant but false freedom. There would have been no need for Judas, who lived in the darkness, and all the drama and crucifixion, but at the same time there would be no resurrection and salvation".

I reflected aloud, "Maybe that is why we have this story in the Bible: so we can see the effects of the devil's work. By being faithful to Mama Kankarra, Jesus shows us that to be faithful is the foundation for our choices. Being faithful to God and to our very selves, or not, is what makes choices moral or not".

I continued. "Because Jesus did pass the test, continued His mission and His work on earth, He freed us from the past and opened the heavens. And when He had accomplished everything, He was ready to go back to Mama Kankarra. So He invited the Apostles and 'Then he led them [out] as far as Bethany, raised his hands, and blessed them. As he blessed them he parted from them and was taken up to heaven. They did him homage and then returned to Jerusalem with great joy, and they were continually in the temple praising God.'" (Luke 24:50-53).

"Sometimes I wonder why, knowing Jesus' story, I continue to have doubts and fears. The Apostles went to the world to share the love and peace and what they learned from Jesus with no fear or doubts. They paid the ultimate price for it; they died for it.

"Why do I lose heart in keeping up His mission, my mission, my own spiritual journey? Why do I allow the darkness to overtake my journey?"

"I heard a story about a very cold country some time ago from a European missionary", started the old man. "I do not understand some of the words and the meaning behind it, but it is an interesting story about a British expedition to the Arctic Ocean. The participants loaded their two ships with all the equipment one might find in a posh London club. There was excellent china, engraved silverware, cut crystal, but the men took only enough coal for twelve days. Their ships became locked in the unforgiving Arctic ice. After many weeks, the desperate crew attempted to walk to safety. All perished. Two officers died near their sled. Their would-be rescuers found they had been dragging sixty five pounds of table silver. (Annie Dillard in Teaching a Stone to Talk)

"Before you headed toward Kumanjayi Springs (Alice Springs), you packed your car and got ready for the journey. Because you know the desert and learned from others, you have all things that you need in order to survive. The mob in the story did not know anything about the journey, and they tried to take their world with them, forgetting about the necessities of life.

"I need to carry with me songs to remember where to find water and where to hunt or gather food. As I walk, I sing songs that I learned from old people and I follow the path of waterholes and mangarri. I stay connected to the universe and adopt the songs to the changes in the world. I need to carry who I am and what I have learned in order to get where I am heading, but also remember where I came from so I understand the progress. The mob from the story tried to get to safety, but they did not know where to go and they burdened themselves with the luggage from their comfortable lives. They feared and doubted nature. The combination of these two things killed them, and it can kill spiritually as well.

"A relationship with the environment is something that we are losing these days because of modern technology, because of lack of face-to-face communication, I think", continued the old man sadly. "My mob traditionally embraces and respects the environment, the trees and animals, the bushes and the sand. I am connected to the land, the trees, and nature. When I listen to my spirit I am connected to the universe, things always work out, and I have no need for fear or doubts. The world outside is not against me. I create the worst enemies inside and fear them, and the fear brings doubt. If I follow the path of doubts, I fail".

"Do not let fear confine your life inside a shell of doubt. A turtle never moves until his head is sticking out" (Charles Ghigna), I quoted hesitantly, trying to challenge my own doubts.

Compassion; Words Cannot Embrace It ...

I was getting cold. The clouds had vanished and the sky was clear, but the temperature had dropped significantly. Our blankets kept us a little warm but we needed the fire. With a hand movement, the old man communicated to the boy that they needed some sticks, and he was off. Even in the darkness you can recognize the familiar, I thought. Aboriginal people use a lot of hand and head movement to communicate. It is very fascinating.

"Where are you heading with the boy?" I asked the old man. I thought he was teaching the boy and getting him ready for the Law time.

"We are going to see his family. His uncle passed away and the family is in the sorry camp. He was my cousin".

"I am so sorry", I said, feeling a bit stupid for assuming.

"He rolled over a car", the old man said, "and died in the clinic. There were a few others involved in the accident, but the Royal Flying Doctors flew them to the hospital and they are doing well. A lot of people in the community are angry about the accident". The man's voice was clear and peaceful. "They are not done yet with the custom of sweeping the ground, but they have all moved out of the house to the sorry camp".

"As you know", the old man continued, "the sorry camp is a designated place outside of the community where the people move after the death to show that they are sorry, to show their grief. I remember the sorry camp when my grandfather died. He was the Law man for the region". He stopped and looked in the direction where the boy had gone. "I want the boy to hear the story and learn about sorry camp. Yanama! (Come over here!)" he called to the boy. We could hear him coming back. The boy returned with the sticks and we lit the fire again. It felt nice and warm, and we could see each other better. The light brought us closer. We held our hands out to the flames and enjoyed the warmth.

The old man turned to the boy and said, "We are talking about sorry camp and I would like you to learn about some old ceremonies. So far you have been allowed to be just a boy when someone died and family went through sorry time. Very soon, after you become a man, you will be part of it and you will have some responsibility. I would like to share a story about sorry time after my grandfather died".

"Was he the Law man at that time?" asked the boy.

"Yes, he was the Law man who was responsible for Law ceremonies" the old man replied.

"When the immediate and the extended family learned about his death, they started to make their way to Kururrungku to join together to go through a sorry time. They set up the sorry camp between the creek and the community. The immediate family moved out of the house to sorry camp and some other members of the family moved into the house of my grandfather. I was about nine years old and did not fully understand what was happening. We only took with us a few clothes and some blankets. My family left behind all the possessions of my grandfather to be burnt or distributed among close members of the family. My family never went back to live in the house. Some other family members moved in after a few months. We all stayed in sorry camp, and everyone from the region came to visit with us. Some of the family members joined us in sorry camp and some stayed in the community; it is based on the relationship with the deceased. We all got painted with white paint, our faces, hair, hands and legs. We use white color to express sorrow. We did not eat meat the whole time, only fish and damper. Us kids, we had some lollies sometimes, but my auntie was not happy when she found out. We ate what the adults ate. It went this way for more than three months before the funeral. There was a lot to talk about, I understood little of it, and people just kept coming to Kururrungku. During that time the family planned the burial and discussed family issues, as well as dealing with not yet reconciled situations within the family of the deceased. I think it took so long because the men needed to choose another Law man".

The old man looked at me and asked, "Can I have some coffee, please?"

He had some coffee and continued. "A few days after my grandfather's death, some women swept the ground where he had walked, with leaves. They picked long branches, swept his house and continued on, loudly mourning through the community, sweeping the ground where he had walked: other houses, the store, the school and so on. They also did a smoking ceremony to "wash" themselves and all visitors. For the smoking ceremony they used the leaves with which they had swept the ground. My grandfather's name was not spoken anymore; it became Kumunytjayi. Every person in the community that had the same name, or in some cases even when it sounded like it, is referred to as Kumunytjayi. Their names are dead. They are Kumunytjayi from now on".

When I looked at the old man he was staring at the fire.

"I am trying", the old man continued slowly, "to teach the boy old ways on this journey, but I am also learning new ways and understanding from him. It is a good journey".

"What was his uncle's skin name?" I asked in order to understand how I am related to him based on kinship.

"He was Tjangala", the old man replied, and I realized he was my brother. I told the old man "I am Tjangala as well!" He hugged me. We stayed embraced for a while. His embrace was strong and gentle at the same time. I realized that even though I had never met the deceased I deeply felt sorrow for his family.

"I pray for your uncle", I said, looking at the boy, "that Mama Kankarra takes him up to heaven. 'He is not God of the dead, but of the living, for to him all are alive. (Luke 20, 38) and your uncle will live with him there forever".

The boy said nothing.

The old man spoke. "Death is perhaps the one truly universal truth. We may all have different beliefs and convictions, come from different cultures and speak different languages, but the truth is that we all die.

"For centuries, death has played an important role in understanding the human race. For some it is a gate to the other world and for some, the end of everything, for some it is a part of the journey and for some the end of a journey, for some it is a saving thing that frees them from this world, and for some a necessary step towards the unknown. The importance of death appears to matter more when we are faced with the death of a loved one. Apart from those times, we try not to think about death.

"I know that sometimes death comes slowly, other times fast and unexpectedly. But we all know it is inevitable. That awareness influences many of our choices and decisions, and colors everything we do, every attitude we assume. To a deep degree it is also true that a person's ability to build a life with purpose and meaning is built on the ability to see purpose and meaning in death. The older I get, the more questions come to my mind about the meaning of life. What defines my life and what do I expect to experience after death?

"What is behind the choices I make? Do I see more than the end of my life? Where would I like to spend eternity? What is the ideal 'world for eternity'? I wonder about these things a lot".

"I do not know the answers, but I know I will miss my uncle a lot", the boy whispered. "He was a good man".

The old man hugged the boy and said, "I am going to miss your uncle very much too. He was a great hunter and a wise man". They sat, embraced in silence, while I added some more sticks to the fire and some sparks flew up.

"We are going to show our compassion to the family in the sorry camp and the community on this sad journey", said the old man. "We are going to show them that we love and care about them. Compassion is the language of love and understanding.

"People who show compassion act on behalf of angels whom we cannot see. Compassion means to be passionate about other people. Compassion guides your mind to love and believe in who is above and those here on earth, other beings. Tjiitju teaches us the same. "Be compassionate just as your Father is compassionate. Do not judge, and you will not be judged; do not condemn, and you will not be condemned; forgive, and you will be forgiven. Give, and there will be gifts for you: a full measure, pressed down, shaken together, and overflowing, will be poured into your lap; because the standard you use will be the standard used for you". (Luke 6:36-38). When I hear it I think to myself every time: It is so simple, really and yet so hard to live by since it is hard to find compassion at work in me".

"I would like to share a gardia story with you", I said.

"We call your mob white people or we call them *whitefella*", said the old man, chuckling.

"Once upon a time there was a very, very old man", I said. "His eyes had grown dim and his ears deaf, and his knees shook when he walked. When he sat at the table, he could scarcely hold a spoon. He spilled soup on the tablecloth and, besides that, some of his soup ran back out of his mouth.

"His son and his son's wife were disgusted with this, so finally they made the old grandfather sit in the corner behind the stove, where they gave him his food in an earthenware bowl, and not enough food at that. He sat there looking sadly at the table, and his eyes grew moist. One day his shaking hands could not hold the bowl, and it fell to the ground and broke.

"The young woman scolded, but he said not a word. He only sobbed. Then for a few half-pence they bought him a wooden bowl and made him eat from it. Once when they were all sitting there, the little grandson of four years pushed some pieces of wood together on the floor.

"'What are you making?' asked his father.

"'Oh, I'm making a little trough for you and mother to eat from when I'm big.'

"The man and the woman looked at one another and then began to cry. They immediately brought the old grandfather to the table, and always let him eat there from then on. And if he spilled a little, they did not say a thing". (The Old Grandfather and His Grandson, by Jacob and Wilhelm Grimm).

"I heard that story at my school", the boy exclaimed, "and we talked about what compassion means. I learned that Mama Kankarra wants me to have a far different model for my relationships. The model is of a constant, mutual gift-giving, the model not of a contract but of covenant. I did not understand it at first, but I read stories about how God keeps on loving people no matter what silly things they do and how God keeps His promises of loving them no matter how much they hurt Him. They call it a covenant in the Bible, a promise that will not be broken no matter what.

"It helps me to have relationships in which what I want to give is not limited by the things that I expect to get in return. I want my character to flow from the understanding that people are holy and good because all people are Mama Kankarra's and God is good.

"I believe I can understand that if I show compassion to others it is because God loves them and they are His kids. I also believe that my character, my morality, is not a matter of what I do, but of what I am".

"So wisely spoken", I said. "I believe that compassion is shown by kindness and 'You can never do a kindness too soon, for you never know how soon it will be too late'. (Ralph Waldo Emerson). I try to be kind every day; I'm not good at that, but I keep trying. I like what you said about doing, and I realized that it is more important who I am deep down even though I fail to show my kindness so many times. But I am on the right track to get it one day, I hope.

"I am human though. I *choose* to be compassionate, or not to. I *choose* the time and the circumstances. I become the judge of who deserves my compassion and when. This is wrong. I am able to excel or limit, grow or regress, learn or grow ignorant, by the choices I make, the many relationships I enter into, the daily decisions that also affect others and promises I give and do not keep. All of these are made at a certain time and affect the future. For all of these I am responsible now and in the future.

"There is a big city in America called New York. I visited that place once and while walking the streets I noticed a building that wears a plaque that reads, 'The only limits to our future are the ones we impose on ourselves.' And I believe that is so true".

"You have travelled the world and learned things from others", said the old man. "You have touched other cultures and I am grateful for you and that you share your encounters. I am able to learn about other places and what other people think and how they live.

"Since you talked about compassion, I know a story about it and would like to share it with you. Not sure where I heard it, but it is a good story.

"I am going to tell you about a runaway kid who was mean and selfish but learned to ask forgiveness.

There was a father who had two sons. One of them decided to get his share from his father and leave, so he insisted on being paid the money he thought he deserved, and he left for another place. He started partying and spending the money. He wasted his money on bad things and in a short time was left with nothing. So he decided to get a job. But because he was not educated or experienced at any work besides farm work with his father, the only job he found was feeding and tending pigs. He was so hungry and miserable that he started to think about going back home. The more he thought about it the more he felt shame. This stopped him from going back.

"One day he felt so hopeless that he started to head back home. He thought about the things to tell his father and his brother to convince them to take him back. But he didn't have to. 'While he was still a long way off, his father caught sight of him, and was filled with compassion. He ran to his son, embraced him and kissed him.' (Luke 15:20) The son asked his father's forgiveness and his father gave him more than that. He gave him his unconditional love.

"His brother was watching and he got very angry with his father for forgiving his selfish brother. He did not even want to come closer and say "Hi", or welcome his brother. He walked off to keep working on the farm, angry and bitter. He walked into the darkness while the father and his son, who had learned compassion, enjoyed the light and the company of others.

"To forgive is not simply to give justice; it is more than justice and the temptation to pay back with the same hurt. It is more than I am capable of; it is God's gift. Compassion brings out the best in the person who gives and the person who receives. Compassion is the universal language of the angels".

And slowly, with his eyes closed, the old man said,

"I hope you have experienced in your life forgiveness.
I hope you know what it is to be loved unconditionally.
I hope you have been kissed and hugged out of true love.
I hope you have cried and felt the salty taste of tears after returning to love.
I hope you can forgive.
I hope you can join in and celebrate forgiveness.
I hope you can rejoice while others are forgiven.
I hope you can choose to love and be forgiven.
I hope you can choose to be free of the past.
I hope you can know compassion".

While he was still talking, I visited my heart, and I prayed to live a risky life, knowing unconditional love. "Every time we make the decision to love someone, we open ourselves to great suffering, because those we most love cause us not only great joy but also great pain. The greatest pain comes from leaving. When the child leaves home, when the husband or wife leaves for a long period of time, or for good, when the beloved friend departs to another country or dies … the pain of the leaving can tear us apart. Still, if we want to avoid the suffering of leaving, we will never experience the joy of loving. And love is stronger than fear, life stronger than death, hope stronger than despair. We have to trust that the risk of loving is always worth taking". (Henri J.M. Nouwen).

"It is so sad that the brother did not share the father's joy", the boy uttered. "I get jealous of other people too. I can see now how I can hurt others and myself by doing that. Why are we so jealous and hateful when others are forgiven and loved?"

"It is truly sad", the old man said, "and it does happen so often in my culture. If anything happens to anyone there is always someone to be blamed for it. After we decide who is to be blamed the next step is "payback" so the person is "justly" punished— paid back. There are talks already about who should be blamed for the recent death of my cousin.

"I remember the first gardia missionaries around the time of the WWII. When they came here to the desert they told us stories from the Bible. One of them was a story about the first people on earth. When they picked and ate that fruit from the tree, there was nobody willing to take responsibility for it. The man said it was the woman's fault and the woman blamed the snake. They did wrong, but did not want to take responsibility. So Mama Kankarra decided to chase them all from His place. Sometimes I worry that Mama Kankarra is going to give it to us for trying to do His job in finding who is to be blamed".

"What we have to realize is that we do not have to find the victim anymore, we do not have to find whose fault it is, because Mama Kankarra sent us Tjiitju and after He died on the cross all the blame and shame was taken away. Jesus paid already for all of us. What we have to do is simply say 'I am sorry, forgive me,'" I said.

"That is so true", the old man responded, "and I know it, but we still try to find the blame with others even though sometimes it is an accident, sometimes it is a mistake, sometimes the person who is dead caused it. So it is very unfortunate that in spite of all of this, we have to find someone who will pay for somebody's death and the only thing we do is to bring more anger and hate.

"At the same time, we have a lot of justice done our old way. For some things there is punishment, and it helps our people to believe that their culture is strong and that justice will be done. I remember a long time ago, I saw two women hitting each other in the middle of the community. I was visiting Balgo and did not know the women, but I understood the process. They were using rocks to cause bleeding so the rest of the mob could see that the justice was being done. They were holding the rocks in their hands and hitting each other's forehead. Everyone in the community was just doing their normal stuff. I do not remember what caused the argument, but I think one of them was 'jealousing' the other over a man. So while they were carrying out their ancient way of justice, a gardia woman saw them and decided to put a stop to the fight. She told them that Mama Kankarra is not happy with them fighting and hurting each other. They stopped at that instant, but the process of reconciliation between the two women was not done. The justice was put aside by someone who did not understand the culture. Years after that abrupt stop, I heard that the women met in Halls Creek, and after drinking a lot they started fighting and one stabbed the other. It was as if no time had passed. The ritual was finished. Unfortunately, one killed the other.

"It makes me sad to even talk about it now. I still wonder if they remembered what the argument was about years later. If the reconciliation process is stopped by someone who is not part of the culture it could end up badly or the people involved might never heal. I learned from this story to be more careful when coming in between people's reconciliation.

"I believe that every act of forgiveness, no matter how it is done, helps one person to move on and unshackles the other person. When two people refuse to be reconciled, that means two people are going backwards instead of moving on with their lives. The time living without being reconciled is a time of living in the past with the hurt, pain or anger. How sad are the lives of people who are living in the past. It makes me very sad. I never hold people in the prison of the past, not forgiving them. I have no right to hold them back, do I?"

"I agree with you on that", I said. "I learn every day to rejoice with and for people who reconcile. 'In just the same way, I tell you, there will be rejoicing among the angels of God over one sinner who repents.' (Luke 15:10). Forgiveness is so powerful that it can change someone's life. I have been forgiven a lot and I know one thing: that I try not to hurt again if I know that someone who forgives me does it because of unconditional love.

"Forgiveness helps one find one's soul and freedom. In the story I told earlier, the father rejoiced and they had a great party. Things are much better than before if I take part in the forgiveness. Forgiveness is a reason for celebration. What was broken is now not simply mended, it is strengthened, renewed. It is a thing to be celebrated.

"It is too easy to limit our understanding of the mercy of God to nothing more than forgiveness of sin. It is a great deal more than that. God's mercy is His divine love poured out for us no matter what we do and where we are. His mercy is the most reliable and constant thing we can imagine. His great mercy is the most powerful force to bring life where is death, to bring joy where is despair, to bring peace where is fear, to bring love where is indifference".

"Sidney Carter, in his song 'Lord of the Dance', offers us a picture of God that I like to reflect on", I continued. "I danced in the morning when the world was begun. I danced on the moon, the stars, and the sun. I came down from heaven and danced on earth... 'Dance,' said He... 'I lead you wherever you may be. I lead you all in the dance,' said He". Perhaps I should invest in patent leather dancing pumps, black tie, and tuxedo, and have them buried with me", I said to my soul.

The boy asked, "Maybe the other son could not rejoice because he did not love his father and his brother?"

"I do not know", I answered, "but it is possible. 'the one to whom little is forgiven, loves little.' (Luke 7:47). Maybe he was so good in his own opinion that he did not do anything wrong and was never forgiven?

"But I know one thing; that I do forgive those I love deeply and truly. It gets harder with those I do not love as I should. I know that to forgive means to allow people to love and learn how to be loved. Forgiveness is freedom to live and be happy. The better I get at forgiveness, the more people around me would be able to love. The greater the forgiveness, the greater the love, so if I want to be surrounded by love, I need to forgive and love big time".

Pray Big. Think Big. Believe Big. Act Big.
Dream Big. Work Big. Give Big. Forgive
Big. Love Big. Laugh Big.

"You talked about justice and the importance of reconciliation", I said, turning to the old man. "The Lord said, 'Pay attention to what the dishonest judge says. Will not God then secure the rights of his chosen ones who call out to him day and night? Will he be slow to answer them? I tell you, he will see to it that justice is done for them speedily. But when the Son of Man comes, will he find faith on earth?'" (Luke 18:6-8)

"I think there is nothing more persistent in all of human history than God's love for you and me. There are many examples and stories to learn about it. There are also a lot of stories about how people have not been particularly lovable. So many times the reasonable, understandable thing for God to do would have been to simply give up, as I see it. But He didn't. God's love is changeless, persistent, and constant. It does not depend on what we do. God's attitude towards us is not a reaction to how lovable and valuable we make ourselves. It is an action, a verb, a thing to do. It is the fruit of a decision He has made since the very beginning about how lovable and valuable we are. He has kept His promise". And I added this quote, "'A soul without regular prayer is a soul without a home. Weary, sobbing, the soul, after roaming through a world festering with aimlessness, falsehoods, and absurdities, seeks a moment in which to gather up its scattered life in which to call for help without being a coward. Such a home is prayer.' Abraham Joshua Heschel (Moral Grandeur and Spiritual Audacity: Essays)

The old man responded, "Prayer and meditation are wonderful things for our souls. It is good, as you said, to make a home with God; our own very personal and intimate home where we talk with God and He talks with us.

"But if I do not have faith, would I ever build a house to invite a guest that I do not believe in? "Would I ever build a house if today I believe and tomorrow I do not?

"I need strong faith to believe in God and accept Him. Faith without consistency is really no faith at all, and I need a consistency that goes far beyond what is most considered to be reasonable and understandable. A consistency of attitude, which, like God's own, does not depend on how I am treated, but which depends rather on a decision I make as to what that attitude should be. And if I do that, then my persistence finally becomes faith.

"I watched once a fight between two men. One of them said a prayer before the fight. Someone from behind me asked, "Will that help him?"

"Yes". I replied, "If he can fight".

"Faith is like a skill that I learned to master. It is first a gift from up above, but I must practice it every day. With strong faith comes the understanding that Mama Kankarra loves me in a different way than people do. I used to think that God loves me like my mum or brothers or other people but I was wrong. I think one of the most challenging truths from the very beginning of time is the fact that God loves us. We can accept God's love. We do believe that God loves people. We even believe that God's love forgives, but our definition of love is shaped by what we know about others and how we would deal with them or treat them.

"We tend to take God's love and try to fit it within our limited hearts by our own stories and experiences, instead of letting God stretch our hearts to allow the growth. It could be painful, but it is necessary to let our hearts grow by expanding the definition of love and forgiveness as unconditional".

"I think I heard a story about a little man," said the boy, "who believed that God loves him. His name was Zacchaeus. One day Jesus was about to come to the village where he lived. The man was very short and wanted so much to see Jesus so he ran ahead and climbed up a sycamore tree so he could see him.

When Jesus came to that spot, he looked up and said, 'Zacchaeus, come down quickly, for today I must stay at your house.' And he came down quickly and received him with joy. (Luke 19:5-6) and Jesus forgave him everything and the man was changed forever. He had done wrong but he believed that God can forgive and he believed that God's love is bigger than his sins and the wrong he has done. Zacchaeus was blessed with strong faith that allows Mama Kankarra's unconditional love".

"There was a man in Jesus' time who was telling people to believe and change. His name was John", I said. "'He went throughout [the] whole region of the Jordan, proclaiming a baptism of repentance for the forgiveness of sins.'"(Luke 3:3)

The old man said, "I might listen to a lot of wise and saintly people through my whole life, but unless I decide to change and grow, nothing will happen. Do not get me wrong, I need wise and holy people on my life paths, but at the end of the day it is my choice to change. As far as I know only babies welcome change". He looked at me with a grin on his face and we both chuckled. "Good one", I said.

"There is a story I like to share with young people as they prepare for the Law (initiation time), so they can understand that nobody can make them change until they decide to do so". (An Old Cherokee Tale of Two Wolves, adapted for Australia)

And the old man told us, "There is a battle that goes on inside people". He said, "The battle is between two 'dingoes' inside us all. One is evil. It is anger, envy, jealousy, sorrow, regret, greed, arrogance, self-pity, guilt, resentment, inferiority, lies, false pride, superiority, and ego.

"The other is good. It is joy, peace, love, hope, serenity, humility, kindness, benevolence, empathy, generosity, truth, compassion and faith".

The young boy thought about it for a minute and then asked the old man, "Which dingo wins?"

The old man simply replied, "The one you feed.

"I think each and every one of us has these two dingoes running around inside us. The evil dingo or the good dingo is fed daily by the choices we make with our thoughts. What you think about and dwell upon will appear in your life and influence your behavior.

"We have a choice: feed the good dingo and it will show up in our character, habits and behavior positively. Or feed the evil dingo, and our whole world will turn negative; like poison, this will slowly eat away at our soul.

"The question is 'Which are you feeding today'?

"I choose to change. I make the choice every day because there are many challenges in my life: the daily challenges that demand my time, money, pride, talents, privacy, sleep.

"If I decide to change tomorrow or the next week I might be wasting my life, or it might be too late to change, so I decide every day. If I am not honest with myself, the change and growth does not happen. Before I change I ask questions. And I pray often to have peace in my heart in order to see the challenges and struggle as opportunities and stepping stones instead stumbling blocks.

"I ask the Spirit of truth to help me see them as a way to grow in perfection and touch the world with my gifts with goodness and love. After all, the only things we ever really own are the things we give away with love".

Is it fair what I am being challenged with?

Am I being taken advantage of?

Am I too generous with my "giving and doing for others"?

How do I view my challenges?

Do I see them as struggles that become part of my life or undeserved burdens?

Do I see them as opportunities for the giving of gifts and growing?

Are they a stumbling block or a stepping stone for me?

"Why do I have to change and grow every day, anyway?" I asked, furrowing my eyebrows. "Growth requires change, and I like certainty. I like to understand yesterday, today, and tomorrow. Certainty makes things more approachable and easier to understand," I said.

The old man looked at me with his eyes wide open, and said, "You are Mamangku, Mama Kankarra with us. We look up to you for guidance and wisdom. What you said is a version without faith because a person with faith approaches the changes of life with the conviction that it is a good thing, that it has a purpose. It was meant to be like that. The Great Creator designed it. That conviction then becomes an attitude towards life and the movement starts and movement is an undeniable fact of life.

"My spirituality, my mind and things I learn, my feelings and emotions, my physical appearance, all of these are constantly subject to change. There is a long way, though, between knowing it and accepting it. So I ask these questions and try to be as frank with myself as possible when I ask them, knowing that I do change.

What makes it easier for me to accept and even welcome the movement, the transformation?

What makes it possible for me to take the next step without fear?

Why does it make me afraid to step into the future being transformed?"

"Transformation can be very hard to understand", I started saying, "and even those who walked with Jesus for a long time did not understand the meaning of it at first. 'As they were about to part from him, Peter said to Jesus, "Master, it is good that we are here; let us make three tents, one for you, one for Moses, and one for Elijah." But he did not know what he was saying.' (Luke

9:33). Transformation requires movement but they wanted to stay and enjoy the past instead of moving on.

"Where do I fail in my understanding of growth?" I asked the old man.

To my amazement the boy tuned in, even though he had looked like he was not listening. "Accept that tomorrow will be different than today, and admit that yesterday was different than today", the boy said. "Seasons change here in the desert. We enjoy the wet season and look forward to the dry season. Each one of them is different and yet they complement each other. We need the seasons in order to have a full cycle of life.

"There are many things in the desert showing me that change is good. I have learned from desert frogs to adapt and change in order to survive. Nature is unpredictable and the seasons do not always look the same. One year could have a good wet season and the next, not enough rain, or it might come late, making the dry season very long. I live in the desert and I am not going to move out of the desert every time nature decides to change the rules. I choose to change and adapt, being grateful for the land and the heavens above.

"The desert frog is well adapted to desert conditions. It can spend years buried deep underground with its glands under the skin full of water. When it feels the rain coming, it digs itself to the surface.

"I got lost one time in the desert, far away from home, and frogs helped me to survive. My mum had taught me to stomp the ground to imitate thunder and rain coming down, to trick the frogs. When they started to surface, I caught them and drank their stored water.

"I noticed that I adapt and change easier when I am forced to, because normally I would not be drinking water stored inside frogs. Necessity is the mother of invention and change sometimes".

"I was thinking, Mamangku", the old man said thoughtfully, "about Jesus' story. I think that the apostles did not understand it at that time because it was not a very personal experience even though they were there".

"I do not understand", I said, puzzled.

"What they saw was something that they could relate to with very limited understanding. It was too big for them at that time. They did not know the future because they did not have strong hope yet. Being with Jesus every day and being part of His story obstructed their understanding of the bigger picture. I feel that you are ready to make some changes in your life, but you are so much in 'now' that it hinders your understanding of your life. Even though you say you know where you come from, I do not think you fully understand how you ended up 'here and now'. This is my observation.

"When I come across an opportunity for change, I have two choices how to look at it.

First way is the present time connected to the past. I look at the challenge and try to understand why, by analyzing the reasons behind the need for change. What causes the change or challenge?

Second approach is present time connected to the future, and since I cannot change the future, I have to have hope. The virtue of hope comes and makes it very personal.

"I believe Mama Kankarra is working with me right here and now. I have a personal relationship with God. But hope is not certainty, and it can be scary. There are a couple of 'if's' attached, and not only do I have to answer them but I also live through them.

"Hope is not passive but active, and it allows me to look forward without fear, if I understand it. This will always work if I open myself to the changes and transformation. It will never work if I grab onto my past".

When you find your definitions in God, I quoted silently, you find the very purpose for which you were created. Put your hand into God's hand, know His absolutes, demonstrate His love, present His truth and the message of redemption and transformation will take hold. (Ravi Zacharias)

"Why did you come here to the desert?" the boy asked me.

"I needed to change. I knew it deep down, but I could not even begin, where I lived. Whenever I told myself, 'You have to change and stop compromising yourself", I would stick with it for a few days or a week and then fall back into the same pattern. I felt like I was living on the surface and never going any deeper with my life. I was rigid and rude because I was frustrated. I became an arrogant and was not nice to people. Arrogance is a state in which you defend yourself without taking any responsibility for your actions and words. Whatever you do is justified by the reasons for the defense. Ultimately you are always right because you have to prove to yourself that you are not guilty or at fault. I lost touch with my soul.

"Mama Kankarra called me many times to leave my country, and after so many years I finally did, still not knowing what to expect, but following God's call. As they were proceeding on their journey someone said to him, "I will follow you wherever you go". (Luke 9:57). I guess this is what I did, decided to follow Him, and He led me into the desert where I am finally facing who I truly am.

"I had to pack everything in two bags and cross the oceans as well as the boundaries of my comfort zone; I did not speak

English, I did not know the culture of Australia and I did not even know about your mob. Where I come from, we have four seasons and different food and culture. I jumped, so to speak, into the unknown, but Mama Kankarra promised to be with me and I trusted Him. That is why I am here. No looking back!

"And I know some more stories about people stepping into the unknown future that you might like", I said to the boy.

"Tell me the stories", the boy said.

"'The Sound of Music' is a true story about the von Trapp family. The time is the late 1930's. The Third Reich marches across Europe. It is not a fun time in Europe for many people. Baron von Trapp is a wealthy man, and he is a former captain in the Austrian Navy. Now he's being recalled to serve the Nazi cause. But he refuses, because he does not agree with what they stand for. He packs up his wife and his seven children, and with only the clothes on their backs, they hike across the Alps to freedom. No looking back!

"Albert Schweitzer, by his early thirties, gains world-wide recognition as a theologian, (a person who studies about God), and he is a professional organist. He learns of the desperate need for medical doctors in central Africa and decides to go to medical school. He raises money to open a clinic in the country of Gabon. For the rest of his life, Albert Schweitzer treats the sick in a poor village in a remote corner of Africa. He never regretted his decision. No looking back!

"There are many more stories like that about people who followed their hearts and souls. I always find stories like that fascinating. I feel that there is something that goes far beyond my ability to experience it all. And because of that, I have the freedom and power to respond to Him beyond my limitations and imagination. I decided this is what I am, this and nothing else. This is what my life means. It is the point in a person's life at which one stops being at the mercy of the moment, of whatever influence is strongest right now, and begins to act in spite of such influences rather than because of them. It is truly a moment of freedom, in the deepest sense. And when it happens, miracles follow".

"Good stories, and easy to understand", the old man said, and continued, "I sometimes struggle with some of the stories from the Bible. They seem to be too complicated. Here is one I struggle with and would like you to help me understand: 'And he told them this parable: "There once was a person who had a fig tree planted in his orchard, and when he came in search of fruit on it but found none, he said to the gardener, 'For three years now I have come in search of fruit on this fig tree but have found none. [So] cut it down. Why should it exhaust the soil?' He said to him in reply, 'Sir, leave it for this year also, and I shall cultivate the ground around it and fertilize it; it may bear fruit in the future. If not you can cut it down.' (Luke 13:6-9) You see, I have never been a gardener and I do not know much about gardening, but if a plant does not produce anything this year or the next, then nature will take care of it, so why cut it down?"

"With this story Jesus teaches me about repentance", I said.

"That is a big word. I have heard it but what does repentance really mean?" the boy asked.

"What does it look like to you when you think about repentance?" The old man added.

"We talked about transformation and movement", I began. "Either one of them could be compromised by the lack of repentance or reconciliation. When the past is holding me back I cannot move forward. I am stuck or moving backwards. Many times when I hear the word repentance I automatically think about the sin or wrong that I have committed. So I focus my energy on trying to bring them to my mind, feel sorry for doing wrong, and avoid it next time. I am so focused on sin. I keep trying and trying over and over again to get better, but I rarely succeed because I focus on things that I have no control over instead focusing on my very self. "Chronic remorse, as all the moralists are agreed, is a most undesirable sentiment. If you have behaved badly, repent, make what amends you can and address yourself to the task of behaving better next time. On no account brood over your wrongdoing. Rolling in the muck is not the best way of getting clean". (Aldous Huxley). But I keep rolling in the muck over and over again.

"Now, if I use my energy in a positive way to change my ways and move into the future, I will be successful. This process is called *metanoia*. It is a Greek word that means a change of heart, change of mind, becoming something new.

"Let us stand up for a moment. I would be able to explain it better, I hope".

We all stood up. The boy and the old man looked at me with big eyes.

"Turn your back to the fire and look ahead. What do you see?" I asked.

"I can see darkness", the boy answered. "I am blocking the light".

"I see my shadow", the old man said.

"I do too", the boy exclaimed.

"I cannot see either one of you", I continued. "I see only my shadow and the darkness. Let us turn around and face the fire". They turned around. "What do you see now?"

"I see the fire and your faces", said the boy, "I am not alone with my shadow and darkness anymore".

"Making the decision to turn away from the darkness and your own shadow is called *metanoia*. It is one's free and conscious decision to change by turning one's own life around. It is turning away from sin and turning towards the light. Not wasting one's time and energy alone by looking at the shadow of sins and darkness inside but turning to the Light and not being alone anymore.

"I do not concentrate on sin but go far beyond my guilt and feeling sorry, into the understanding that doing good can bring me joy. *Metanoia* is a big and important word to remember and practice. I hope I helped you understand the story. I also ask these questions occasionally:

How many times have I done the same bad things over and over again?

How much energy and time have I spent in trying to avoid sinning or making the same mistakes I've made before?

Am I not tired yet of experiencing the same thing and getting disappointed with myself?

"I am called to live a good life and not just to avoid sin in my life! This attitude helps me put more energy into doing good instead of avoiding evil. 'We cannot forever go on being a good egg. Some day we have to hatch'". (Evelyn Underhill.)

"Do you have your spiritual plan?" the old man asked me. "Many gardia people are known for making business plans or writing their personal development plans for the years to come".

"I do not have a plan", I answered. "I know that 'All you have to do is to pay attention; lessons always arrive when you are ready, and if you can read the signs, you will learn everything you need to know in order to take the next step' (Paulo Coelho), but it is a long way from knowing it to putting it into practice. I think I am turning around to see the Light again, but I do not have a plan. I know the words, "Be vigilant at all times and pray that you have the strength to escape the tribulations that are imminent and to stand before the Son of Man". (Luke 21:36) and years from now, five, or ten, if I have taken the next step, if I have been faithful, if I have waited with hope, then I shall be made complete. But I do not have a plan".

The old man nodded and said, "I knew a wise Law man who lived at Kururrungku. Young boys would ask him questions about things.

"One day my grandson asked him, 'What has life taught you, Law man? Did you become good?'

"'Not at all', answered the Law man.

"'Did you become wise?' the boy questioned.

"'Not at all', the law man said. 'I still learn a lot.'

"'What then has life taught you?' The boy did not give up.

"'I became awake and aware of things that I need to learn and improve', replied the Law man.

"You mentioned standing before the Human One", the old man continued, turning to me. "Did you mean God?"

"It refers to our final destination, heaven, going back to Mama Kankarra. Remember the one who was crucified with Jesus when he said, 'Jesus, remember me when you come into your kingdom. 'He replied to him, 'Amen, I say to you, today you will be with me in Paradise.' (Luke 23:42-43) I believe this means to stand before the Human One up above in heaven, called paradise".

"What is paradise?" the boy asked with a curious voice.

"I believe", I said, "that I am a pilgrim in this world. I travel through time and space. I journey. Hopefully, I journey with a purpose. My faith helps me to successfully deal with the mystery of life. Nothing can take faith's place. Because of faith I know that the world is not mine. I know I am a guest with a purpose. I am not a wanderer, but a pilgrim.

"I believe your mob used to be called nomads. They always travelled with a purpose, following the seasons and food. Like a nomad, I know where I am heading and my journey is purposeful. I might not remember it always or understand it at times, but I can choose the path to it, the path to paradise. And for different people, the word paradise can mean different things.

"For some it looks like the Garden of Eden where God walks and lives with people in harmony, but they focus more on here and now. They understand that they have to prepare themselves to be close to the Perfect One.

"For others it looks like a walled garden or park. They get there on the fourth day after death by crossing the Bridge of the Separator, which widens when the good people approach it. The good souls cross the bridge and are met by a beautiful maiden who is the physical and feminine representation of all their good works on earth. They walk into the House of Song to await the Last Day. On this day, everyone will be made clean and live in a new world, free of evil and full of youthful rejoicing. And that is their paradise.

"Others understand paradise as a place where the souls sing and rejoice before God. It is also called New Jerusalem and it has a wall and twelve gates, and on each gate is the name of one of the tribes of Israel along with an angel. There are also twelve foundations. It is built out of all kinds of precious stones, some of which we do not even know yet. There is a flowing river with "the water of life," and trees of life grow on the banks. Everyone in this paradise lives with God, and all pain, tears, and death will disappear forever.

"Yet another vision of paradise is this: Your good works must be heavier than the bad ones, as explained in the Quran. Paradise is a beautiful garden with comfortable places to sit down accompanied by beautiful virgins. They will drink from crystal and silver vessels. Those who are in this paradise will be very well clothed, wearing jewelry, and will be rewarded for their striving and patience.

"And there are a few different images of paradise where it is offered as a kind of release from illusion and suffering in the present world. They believe that, because they live in this world, their actions connect them to this world, which is in fact illusory. If they learn and grow, through karma they can free themselves and be released from illusion and suffering, reaching the state of moksha, or their paradise.

"Similar is the next religion. What keep these next people in illusion is their desires: desire to have and desires to be. The desires cause suffering and burn them and keep them within the circles of their egos, keep them tied to the cycle of death and rebirth. Nirvana is the state of paradise, or the extinguishing of the flame that burns them, which is also the end of suffering.

"We can find more images that illustrate what paradise might look like, or mean, to different people, but no matter what I imagine it to look like and feel like for most people in the world, it is the ultimate goal of their journey. And for each one of them it is the most desirable and wonderful place to be".

"And people will come from the east and the west and from the north and the south and will recline at table in the kingdom of God", (Luke 13:29) the old man said unexpectedly. He had been sitting with his eyes closed and a smile on his face. "Everyone is looking for a purpose and meaning in life. It is so hard to go through rough times without a purpose and to cope with suffering without understanding why it exists. 'Why me?' they say".

"Teresa of Avila was, for a while, superior of her order in all of Spain", I shared. "Teresa and her companion were travelling along a lonely dirt road in the middle of the night, in the middle of a rainstorm, in a small horse-drawn wagon. And the wagon got stuck in the mud. So they got out and pushed, and pulled, and finally got it free. But, when Teresa got back up on the wagon to gather the reins, the horse bolted and dumped her unceremoniously in the mud. And as she lay there, sort of gazing up at the sky, according to her companion's report, the only thing that she said was, 'Lord, if this is the way you treat your friends, it is no wonder you have so few of them.'

"Simon of Cyrene was compelled by the Romans to carry the cross of Jesus. He was a bystander who had found himself on the way of the cross by accident. I believe he was one of many who experienced the same. He was given no explanation for carrying Jesus' cross. The only realistic choice he had was to simply put up with it.

"I have experienced on my life journey some unwanted suffering or undeserved 'crosses'. People can suffer physical disease or handicaps, mental or emotional aches and pains, anxiety, loneliness and boredom. They do not invite trouble into their lives. These problems simply seem to come into their lives, and always bring with them the question, 'Why?'

"When I visited Rome, in one of the churches I saw a powerful image of Christ after the resurrection by Michelangelo called 'Cristo della Minerva'. There are two distinct elements to this sculpture, in my opinion. What pops up immediately is Christ. His body here is powerful, strong, beautiful and perfect. But what is truly puzzling and different is the second piece, which is much smaller, lighter, far less powerfully sculpted. It is the cross.

"I was very surprised to see Christ holding His cross after the resurrection. So I asked myself the question, 'Why hadn't he simply cast the hated thing away to show that he is more powerful than the cross?' And I kept looking at the statue and meditating on the message.

"I noticed after a while that Christ was not bearing the cross. In fact he was just barely touching the cross; he held it in His fingertips, with a familiarity, almost a fondness. The tool of torture, suffering, and death was still there, but it was no longer a burden. And what had made all the difference was the resurrection.

"I like that image very much, and it truly helps me put into perspective my own sufferings and aches and pains. It works in my life even though it brings the question, 'Why?'

"And I remind myself often: 'Tell your heart that the fear of suffering is worse than the suffering itself. And that no heart has ever suffered when it goes in search of its dreams, because every second of the search is a second's encounter with God and with eternity.' (Paulo Coelho, The Alchemist)

"I think Jesus always tries to encourage me with his words not to be afraid: 'Whoever does not carry his own cross and come after me cannot be my disciple' (Luke 14:27), because His cross is not a heavy burden but the sign of victory".

As the boy added some sticks to keep the fire going, the old man slowly stood up. He started unbuttoning his shirt slowly, taking it off and showing us his chest. It was covered with many scars. They were cuts on both sides, with no regular pattern. Some of them were longer than others.

"These scars were intentionally put on my chest to tell stories of pain, endurance, identity, status, beauty, courage, sorrow and grief", he said with pride. "It is my mob's way of sharing with others what we have been through in life. Others can read the stories on my body, or I can share the meaning of the scars. Each one of them I gained in different stages of my life. It is a map of my life journey.

"When I was a boy I behaved like a boy, thought like a boy", he said as he put his shirt back on. "My family and my community were safe places to learn and explore what it means to be a person. Otherwise, what makes me different from animals?

"As a child, I was allowed to make many mistakes in order to learn from them. I was forgiven easily and protected by all. I was a child, learning what it means to be a person. I played with everyone, and most of the time I was very happy. The only painful lessons were those I created by bad choices.

"I lost my mum when I was five years old. Her sister became my natural mum and I felt loved the same. There is no adoption in our families because we look after each other. In particular, we look after all the kids no matter who the real mums or dads are. We are all one family here in Kutjungka; we come together and look after each other.

"I was growing happy and slowly getting to a point of taking more responsibility for myself and others. It was time to get ready for *Law*, to become a young man. I spent weeks with old men, hunting and learning stories and learning our culture, and came to understand more and more what it means to be a male. I had to stop sitting close to or playing at school with the girls, and I no longer talked with them before going through *Law*. It was time to learn how to be a man. It was also a time in my life to do silly things, as you remember the boomerang story, because I was still a boy.

"Part of the change and growth between a boy and a man is discipline. I had to be more responsible. I carry my aches and pains of growing in order to learn what the difference is between a female and a male. Some of the scars on my chest are from that time.

"Understanding my manhood required for me to take the next step, namely to find out what I wanted to do with my life, what I wanted to become in life. I needed to learn new skills and gain more scars to understand my path and choose to follow it or not. Growing up is painful and requires getting more and more scars, but that is a wise way of growing. To go from playing to being responsible was not easy at all, but it was necessary; otherwise I would have never grown up and known responsibility. I would have never known love and given love.

"If I rejected every scar that I carry on my chest I would have become indifferent to the world and other people, and that is the opposite of love. Indifference speaks the words that I hear a lot: 'I do not care' and 'whatever'.

"I have been hurt and I have hurt. I have been forgiven and I have forgiven.

"Each time I gain a scar on my chest or on my heart, I live deeper and bigger, and my journey is meaningful because I take responsibility and show love, no matter how imperfect it is. Suffering, for me, is taking responsibility for the journey and following my path".

And as I listened to the man speaking I noticed the similarities between the Aboriginal way of life and my understanding of life and its purpose: "God created man in the image of himself, in the image of God he created him, male and female he created them. God blessed them, saying to them, 'Be fruitful, multiply, fill the earth and subdue it. Be masters of the fish of the sea, the birds of heaven and all the living creatures that move on earth". (Genesis 1:27-28)

"I do not have any scars on my chest", I said, "but a lot on my heart, which has created a map of my failures and successes, my weaknesses and strengths. It has created the map of my soul. Scars caused by others and wounds caused by me. All of the scars are there, hidden from the world and seen by God.

"In your world, you show openly your story to the world and God knows your heart. How differently we live. You live like an open book, showing your scars, I hide things in my culture and build an image with words and sometimes made up stories to 'show' good behavior and be 'an example'.

"Perhaps for some people it becomes a little easier to make their peace with the mystery of suffering if they reflect on what the cross was in the life of Christ. It was not only something that an angry mob did to Him. Much more importantly, it was something that He freely chose to do to Himself. Christ carried the cross for years before the day we call Good Friday.

"As I carry my crosses, I realize that part of the cost of being a good person, understanding what it means to be a male and following my path, must be a readiness to center my life around what is valuable and good, rather than the values of the world, rather even perhaps than the values proposed to me by my own experience. That is very hard, but I have Mama Kankarra's blessing to do it, and with God, I know, everything is possible".

"I told you at the beginning that when I first saw you I knew you are a good man, but with no peace in your heart", the old man spoke. 'You know how to interpret the appearance of the earth and the sky; why do you not know how to interpret the present time?' (Luke 12: 56)

"I have learned from your words that with all your strength you try to find peace. You turn to anything that could provide a good sleep or some relief from the stresses and hectic or even chaotic way of life. You probably try to drink until you fall asleep, watch movies till you get too tired to follow anymore, read books or pray. It worked once or twice or a few times, but does it really work in the long run?

"Just be honest! Usually, instant help does not last, and the 'medicine or procedure' has to be repeated. My guts tell me that you are frantically trying to find a substitute for peace instead of the true peace which you cannot find.

"How about simply facing the reality rather than trying to run from it? You have faith, don't you? Faith helps to face reality as it is. The question is, is your faith strong enough to cope with it?" The old man spoke these words with strong but concerned voice.

I felt called to answer this. "I used to be able to look up at the sky and know the weather. I would look at the moon at night and knew the rain would come in three days. Most of these things my grandfather taught me. As a child, I enjoyed the peace and balance of the universe that I was part of, but I lost the peace. Slowly I started compromising my path and myself. I kept making the same mistakes without learning anything".

I covered my face in my hands and stopped. I did feel like crying but needed to finish sharing.

I took a deep breath and continued slowly, with a calm voice.

"I grew arrogant and self-absorbed. I turned my back on God and the Light. I relied on rules and regulations and put them between me and others. It was easier to deal with people and not take any responsibility for my decisions".

"'The church teaches so', I would say or, 'Jesus said so'. I lost peace in my heart because I denied my identity and integrity. I rejected God as my Lord and adopted some parts of His teaching as a weapon. I equipped myself with the armor of judgment and pride. I lost the balance of the universe and fell into my own trap. I needed a way out, but could not do it for years. So the heavens and the earth brought me here to face the reality of God's unconditional love. When I was a wanderer without a purpose, I surrounded myself with only the 'wisdom' that would fit my convictions, but deep down I knew it was wrong not to walk the path of God but follow my own.

"There were many attempts from up above to get me on track, but I was so selfish that even God was out of my path. I started blaming God for my weak decisions and bad choices. I blamed him for a lot, but deep down, again I felt shame for doing that. It is very common to hide shameful and weak things in my culture, and the scars were not shown to anyone.

"Christians,' said Albert Camus, 'should get away from abstraction and confront the bloodstained face history has taken on today.' When people are troubled, we cry to Christ, 'Why aren't you there?' Christ replies to us, 'Why aren't you?' With my heart of stone at that time, I said those are just some words, nothing more than that.

"I think I did reach a point in my life when, instead of trying to grow out of it, I grew comfortable with the mess in my life, and quite complacent about it. And I remember trying to talk to my soul more frequently than before, but with more pain in my heart, and tears, hidden at night and diluted by alcohol. 'Maybe it is a good time for me to stop trying 'to get the prophet out of our city so we can honor him or onto a cross so we can love him.' as James Carroll puts it," I thought to myself. 'Maybe it is a time for me to invite God to flip my life upside down and build a strong faith foundation. It is never too late to invite Him. It is never too late to start'", I sobbed.

I felt gentle touch on my shoulder and I heard words that sounded like a prayer. The old man held his hand firmly on my shoulder.

The boy confessed, "I talk a lot about changes as well, instead of just making them happen". I looked at the boy and appreciated his confession.

"I do feel your pain and feel your frustration, but I am not sure", the man looked at the boy as he spoke, "if you are ready to have and respect peace yet. You have not mastered yet the art of listening or the art of finding the unexpected.

"The first is needed in order to learn and the second is needed in order to live with undisturbed peace. Are you willing to learn these steps in your life?" he asked.

I nodded, wiping my eyes.

"I have learned all stories and songs to create the map of our land by listening. I had to listen carefully because the songs would describe where I can find water or food. By listening I built up a map of my country, so when I went walkabout and lived in the wilderness, I could survive. It is a matter of life and death sometimes. If I did not listen carefully, I could have been dead. I believe the same applies to my spirit and to building a map in my soul of the 'inner country' that will help me be safe and grow through any experience. I have two ears and one mouth, and I always try to remember that. I try to listen twice as much as I talk.

"To master the art of listening, you need to understand what listening is and the importance of it.

"There was an old Chinese man in Broome who showed me a picture once and said, 'this thing looks funny to you, but it is a letter that means 'to listen''. The old man drew this picture with a stick in the sand.

"On the left side, the long part that looks like a ladder is 'ear'. On the right side on the top, what would say it looks like?"

I guessed. "Eyes".

He said, "Correct".

"Below what looks like eyes there is a sign that means 'undivided attention', and on the right bottom what you see is 'heart'.

"Ear – to listen to the melody of the words and catch the context of what a person is trying to share with me, to hear every word with respect. To pick up the tone of voice and use it to determine if the person is happy or angry.

"Eyes – to see the body language, face expressions, hands and all 'nonverbal words' and communication. It is a very big part of talking with others. When my mouth stops talking, my whole body continues to talk.

"Heart – to listen to the feelings, empathy and sympathy lead me to a better understanding. Listening with a heart means that I have a loving and open attitude and that compassion is my guide.

"Undivided attention – so I can hear every word, see every expression and determine every feeling to show my respect and love, it is a selfless act of giving full attention to another person.

"I believe if I engage all of them I can become a good listener who not only hears every word but understands the meaning behind each one of them. You see, the meaning of the word is not with the word but with the person who expresses the word, as we talked before.

"I carry the meaning of the words I speak. Every word I speak brings the story of my life, the friends I have come across, and the experiences of my life where I tested the meaning of the word. When I say 'I love you', it probably means something different than what you understand when I say it. You and I carry the meaning of the words we speak. The same word can mean something different to you and to me. If that happens we can have a misunderstanding or even an argument or a fight. To avoid these things, we listen and ask questions in order to understand.

"The old Chinese man encouraged me to learn the art of listening, and I have found out that it is the way to find peace and balance inside of me. To listen well, means to me that I pay more attention to others than I pay to myself. It helps me fight my selfishness.

"The other important gift to learn is the art of finding the unexpected. It is the art of living my life without the fear or anxiousness of the unexpected.

"If I want to follow my heart and my dreams, I must be prepared to find the unexpected and not be discouraged by it. Most of the good things that happened to me are unexpected and unplanned by me. If I was not ready to embrace them, I would reject them and maybe even change my path to avoid more surprises like that. I could have walked the safe path of a very comfortable life, but that does not lead to happiness. 'You can become blind by seeing each day as a similar one. Each day is a different one, each day brings a miracle of its own. It's just a matter of paying attention to this miracle.'(Paulo Coelho)

"Whenever I follow my dreams without fear there are unexpected blessings and opportunities waiting for me. Mama Kankarra waits with the right person or the right opportunity. It has always been on His terms, not mine, when I find the unexpected. So I pray for you to learn the art of listening and the art of finding the unexpected. When you master them, you will find peace".

"If you do not expect the unexpected you will not find it, for it is not to be reached by search or trail". (Heraclitus), the ancient philosopher reminded me in my head.

"When I hear the word 'peace'", I said, "I can think of many meanings. It means a great deal more than simply an absence of conflict or war.

"It has positive meaning, first of all. There is peace that means to be restored and made whole again, to be complete. The word for it comes from Hebrew: "Shalom".

"There is peace that means to join together pieces into a whole: wholeness. It means inner peace. The word for it comes from Greek: Eiréné.

"There is peace that means 'peace of mind as the only way to originate a peaceful act'. Shanti is the word and it comes from Asia and is essential to some religions.

"No matter where I look I see the importance of this gift of peace that the world cannot offer, that this world cannot give. 'Into whatever house you enter, first say, 'Peace to this household." (Luke 10, 5).

But what do I say if I do not have peace?

What do I bring to others?

"The opposite of peace is chaos, war, havoc. Is this what I bring instead of peace?

"I remember", I continued, "listening to an interview with a great American poet, Maya Angelou. She recalled a teacher asking her to read a story which ends with the words 'God loves me.' She read the story, closed the book, and the teacher said, 'Read it again.' A little irritated, she read the story again. The teacher said, 'Read it again.' After seven readings, Maya Angelou says she began to feel there really is a God who loves her, deeply and personally.

"That's what I need to share with the world. I would like to share a deep sense of being personally loved by God. The first fruit of realizing that God loves me is deep peace. As long as I believe that 'God loves me', the peace will stay deep in my heart. Peace to be spread in words and deeds as a blessing. I have to find this peace, and the first thing I am to say to the world, the first blessing I am to bring, is 'Peace'".

"Share it joyfully when you find it", said the old man. "It is an unexpected gift, but be prepared to embrace it. It is one of the most amazing gifts a person can have".

We looked at each other and knew that the time arrived to go our separate ways. I looked on the horizon and saw a glimpse of a light. The sun was coming up. What was hidden in the darkness now would be seen in the light.

Sunsets and sunrises are very spiritual experiences in the desert. Their beauty lasts very short, but the memories last very long. The colors of red, orange, pink, yellow and other pastels set the earth apart from the heavens, not to separate them, but to bring the beauty of each one of them into focus. The light brings life and movement again.

The boy came to give me a hug, but the old man said, "Let us sing the blessing song and bless each other for the journey that is ahead".

We held each other by our arms and started to sing:

"May the blessing of our God be upon you; the blessing of the Father and the Son,

And may the Spirit of God, the Spirit of Love be with you all the time".

"Yankula" (Let's go), said the boy. "Yiningku Mama, Yiningku Katja, Yiningku Kurunpa Palya", and they crossed themselves, asking the Trinity to be with them.

I watched them for a while as they disappeared from my sight. They walked to the north. As I saw the sun growing bigger and brighter to my right, the community which I was heading to appeared on my left. I was about half a mile from my destination.

In the light I can see it, but in the dark I could not find it. I decided to sit down and feel the warmth of the rising sun on my face. I was on my own but I did not feel alone. I felt the presence of the angels again, holding me close. I was not afraid anymore. I started to cry uncontrollably.

Living With Contradictions ...
Moving On ...

"Rejoice and leap for joy on that day! Behold, your reward will be great in heaven", (Luke 6:23) I heard in my soul while still crying. What a contradiction, I thought, crying and rejoicing, but I felt my heart growing. It hurt and at the same time felt good. It felt like my heart was shaking off the shackles of comfort and bad habits. It felt like the freeing process of a person who has been squeezed into a very tight box for a long time finally stretching his legs and arms and taking a deep breath. It felt like life inside of me again, after a long time.

I realized that night how broken and wounded I was. For the first time I confronted them with my words in the presence of God and others. I came to understand that a wide variety of feelings are necessary to live life to the fullest and to reach my full potential. Every possible feeling, every virtue or quality of life has contributed to who I am. I am made of mistakes, failures, successes and wins. I simply have to acknowledge them and learn from them.

I have good days and bad days, and sometime very bad days that seem to go on forever. I must always remember God's promise of a meaningful life. Every person, I believe, at some point in her or his life, will mirror the weakness of the human condition, the poverty of life, perhaps physically, economically, emotionally, spiritually. At that very point it is critical to believe that God loves wounded people. No matter what comes in my life, I need to learn to do it well: hopefully, joyfully. Through that process I will be blessed.

As I was putting stuff into my car I was grateful for the darkness so I could appreciate the light even more. I asked myself:

Do I love and respect myself enough so I can find the unexpected?

With a deep sigh I jumped into the car and I was on my way to visit the community.

I knew I had changed that night, but I also knew that it was just the beginning. I looked on the passenger's seat and found a piece of paper with this written on it: "Thank you for allowing me to enter into your stubborn heart and aching soul, after such a long time. Creating the opportunities is my job. Yours are the choices. I love you." God

O my Jesus, I believe in you.
You are my Lord and my God.
I trust you and I love you.
You are the way the truth and the life.
Thank you for all the good things you have given me.
Please look after me and all my family.
Keep us safe and free from harm
And make us truly good, deep in our hearts.
0 my Jesus, I believe in you.
You are my Lord and my God.

O gentle and loving St. Anthony, share my longings and prayers with the Sweet Infant Jesus, who loved to be folded in your arms. Amen.

24179099R00080

Made in the USA
San Bernardino, CA
15 September 2015